An Advent Alphabet

An Advent Alphabet

Daily Readings from William Stringfellow

JEFFREY A. MACKEY

WIPF & STOCK · Eugene, Oregon

AN ADVENT ALPHABET
Daily Readings from William Stringfellow

Wipf & Stock
An Imprint of Wipf and Stock Publishers
199 W. 8th Ave., Suite 3
Eugene, OR 97401

www.wipfandstock.com

PAPERBACK ISBN: 978-1-7252-8136-3
HARDCOVER ISBN: 978-1-7252-8135-6
EBOOK ISBN: 978-1-7252-8137-0

Manufactured in the U.S.A.   11/05/20

Material from the following works by William Stringfellow used with permission of Wipf and Stock Publishers:
   Conscience and Obedience
   Count It All Joy: Reflections on Faith, Doubt and Temptation
   Dissenter in a Great Society: A Christian View of America in Crisis
   Free in Obedience
   My People Is the Enemy: An Autobiographical Polemic
   A Private and Public Faith
   A Simplicity of Faith: My Experience in Mourning
   The Politics of Spirituality

CONTENTS

PREFACE

In my junior year at Nyack College (New York), I was given an assignment by a favorite Bible professor, Don J. Kenyon. I was to read *An Ethic for Christians and Other Aliens in a Strange Land*, by William Stringfellow. It was an extra credit assignment (for which I made request), so I worked intently on reading and reporting. I was "caught" within the first chapter of the book by Stringfellow. Since then I have read every writing of Stringfellow. Providentially, in 1994 I was graciously invited to be a Fellow-in-Residence at the School of Theology of The University of the South in Sewanee, Tennessee. There I spent my time researching Stringfellow, speaking with faculty members who knew him, and addressing several student gatherings. Since that time, I have been privileged to write about him and to have an essay included in Robert Boak Slocum's *Prophet of Justice, Prophet of Life*, a work dedicated to essays on Stringfellow.

Without hesitation I recommend one's reading of all that William Stinrgfellow wrote. Every work of his coheres as one would expect from a good writer with a singular commitment. In one book, *Conscience and Obedience*, his theme is the two Advents of Jesus Christ, the Word of God. But buried within other works are key concepts which have to do with the reality of this Word of God and therefore of Jesus Christ. Here I have endeavored to mine some of that material and arrange it as an Advent reader to aid one in a special time of devotion *before* Christmas begins.

William Stringfellow was born on April 28, 1928 and died on March 2, 1985. An Episcopal lay theologian, a Harvard Law

School–trained lawyer, and a Christian social activist, Stringfellow's theology, his understanding of law, and his public activism were, each and every one, informed and proscribed by his commitment to Jesus Christ as the Word of God, the Lord. He was impatient with easy answers to real-life questions. He concluded that the Word of God is "notoriously active" in the contemporary world, and that the first Advent of Jesus, the Christ, was an act of divine incarnation which, because of its militant battle and final victory over the Fall (which he took as a literal historical reality defining the human person), would necessitate a second Advent when all hope would be sight, all victory manifested, and all righteousness fulfilled. The temporal politics of the world would be defeated indeed, and the permanent politics of the kingdom of God would be eternally and forever present in the created order and King Jesus would rule and reign from the throne.

Stringfellow was not always appreciated during his lifetime, especially by many in his own Church, the Episcopal Church (though many recognized his prophetic gift). He had much to say to the Church and what he said was not easily received and often not digested. He was often not trusted: he was a lawyer and he thought and taught theology without seminary training. His regular and burning words for the Church, which was, by choice, irrelevant to its community and to its own membership, and, more often than not, more interested in the *institution* than in the true *ministry* and *evangelism* of the Church's mandate, were many.

I have chosen Advent-related words which Stringfellow either used or referred to through metaphor or example. Each has its place in the relationship of two Advents of Jesus Christ.

I have maintained his generic "man," "men," and "mankind" so as to not have to rewrite entire sentences. Hear him speaking to all humanity—each and every one of us. I have also remained true to his original capitalization of "Church" at times and not at others—the same holds for "Body of Christ." There is no consistency of capitalization among his many books.

INTRODUCTION

Stringfellow had little patience for Christians who were Christian in words only. One whose conscience had been made alive by bowing the knee to the lordship of Christ must, of necessity, manifest that redemption through conspicuous obedience. Anything less was incongruous with the Word of God.

Approaching Advent, Stringfellow is particularly pertinent to this period of the liturgical calendar in that he saw Advent, the "second coming," as placing men and women in a tension where there is seen a cohesiveness to the Scripture often without a neat "harmonization." He was not what some would call "a date-setter," or "a dispensationalist." He may not have even studied what dispensationalism is. Rather, he calls his reader to find in the Bible "style, not stereotype, for precedent, not model, for parable not proposition, for analogue, not aphorism, for paradox, not syllogism, for signs not statutes. The encounter with the biblical witness is empirical, as distinguished from scholastic, and it is confessional, rather than literalistic; in either case, it is over and above any other consideration, involved the common reader in affirming the historicity of the Word of God throughout the present age, in the biblical era and imminently."[1]

It is this man we will encounter in these readings during Advent. I have taken twenty-three letters of the alphabet as hooks on which to hang Stringfellow's writings which make themselves applicable to Advent and the themes of the first Advent and the

1. Stringfellow, *Conscience and Obedience*, 10–11.

ix

second Advent. There is straight Stringfellow here—and one's Advent will take on new shades of spiritual depth and wonder which few other Advent readers can provide, or even endeavor to provide.

May your Advent be a resounding celebration of the past, a powerful hope for the present, and an unshakable assurance of the second coming as you encounter the Word of God through these writings of William Stringfellow.

Jeffrey A. Mackey
Trinity Sunday 2020
Chapel of St. Dominic, Glen Alpine, North Carolina

WEEK I

SUNDAY

On this first Sunday of Advent, our lives are confronted with two bookends. We have, on the one hand, the first Advent of Christ, which we have given the name Christmas, and which has been adulterated by Western society making it a three-month buying spree when we spend cash in amounts hitherto unknown to human history. Then there is the often soft-peddled or ignored second Advent, which is generally an embarrassment to the contemporary church. This first Sunday of Advent is purposed to make us celebrate the first Advent within sight of the second, and to anticipate the second Advent based on the promises of the first. There is no soft-peddling in Stringfellow and he thrusts us into the doctrine of incarnation quite soon in many of his writings.

"All theology is biography," noted Frederick Buechner. Stringfellow would find dynamic truth and would wholeheartedly agree:

> . . . the theological treatment of biography—and, more broadly, history—to be biblically apropos; after all, the Old Testament is, to a large extent, Israel's story, just as the Gospel accounts tell the story of Jesus and his disciples, while the Book of Acts is biography of the apostles and the other pioneer Christians who became the Apostolic Church. Similar affirmations can be made from the Epistles, and, for that matter, the prisoner's diary which is the Book of Revelation.
>
> The theological exploration of biography or the theological reconnaissance of history are apt, and even normative, styles because each is congruent with the

definitive New Testament insight and instruction: *The Incarnation*. Biblical faith is distinguished from all religions, all philosophies, and all ideologies by the redundant insistence upon the presence and vitality of the Word of God in common history, and Christians particularly confess that the involvement of the Word of God in the life of this world becomes most conscientious, comprehensible, and intentional in the event of Jesus Christ. The historic, incarnate activity of the Word of God signifies the militance of the Word of God, both in cosmic dimensions of space and time and in each and every item of created life, including *your* personhood and *your* biography or mine. It is this same basis of the Christian faith that is so often diminished, dismissed, omitted, or ignored when theology is rendered in abstract, hypothesized, propositional or academic models. There is, then, with the latter something incongruent about the mode of theological discourse—something inherently inappropriate about the method being employed to present the gospel. So, I believe, biography (and history), *any* biography and *every* biography, is inherently theological, in the sense that it contains already—literally by virtue of the Incarnation—the news of the gospel whether or not anyone discerns that. *We* are each one of us parables.

What I am referring to here amounts, of course, to a doctrine of revelation. What I am discussing is how the living Word of God is implicated in the actual life of this world, in all its tumult and excitement, ambiguity and change, in the existence of nations and principalities, human beings and other creatures, in every happening in every place in every moment (cf. Revelation 19:11–16). This world is the scene where the Word of God is; fallen creation—in all of its scope, detail, and diversity—is the milieu in which the Word of God is disclosed and apprehended; Jesus Christ verifies how the Word of God may be beheld by those who have sight and hearing to notice and give heed to the Word of God (cf. John 1:1–14).

Biography, thus, is rudimentary data for theology, and every biography is significant for the knowledge it yields of the Word of God incarnate in common life, whether or not the subject of the biography is aware of that significance of his or her own story. *Vocation* is the name of the awareness of *that* significance of one's own biography. To have a vocation or to be called in Christ means to discern the coincidence of the Word of God with one's own selfhood, in one's own being, in its most specific, thorough, unique, and conscientious sense.[1]

Beginning Advent seems like postponing Christmas for me; I have been often squeezed into the secular mold of beginning Christmas in October and looking to Advent for four Sundays before December 25. Lord God, I need to be forgiven my myopic secularity and I ask that you restore a sense of liturgical, biblical timing to my life. Christmas can wait—I know that; make my confessional statement a reality in my daily, common life. Amen!

---

1. Stringfellow, *Simplicity of Faith*, 19–21.

MONDAY

Advent

*I will put enmity between you [the serpent] and the woman [Eve];
between your brood and hers. They shall strike at your head and you
shall strike at their heel.* (Genesis 3:15)

A new liturgical year has begun for the Church, a year which is
unpredictable as all years are unpredictable, and a year which is
as incalculable as a not-yet-realized fortune. Advent, for all Christians, is as hopeful as hopeful can be in a world which is stuck in
the quagmire of the admixture of fallenness and redemption as redemption wrests victory from the defeated enemies of righteousness; a world which has declared over its existence both its need for
redemption and its redemption as well. Inseparably experiencing
that need for redemption with the reality of its accomplishment,
and its past, present, and future reality as all intensely true at the
same time, makes, for even the most victorious, times of conflic-
tion and times of elation. These are always, so it seems, times of
expectation—of anticipation.

Advent begins with the "A," the letter which anticipates an
entire alphabet. Jesus affirms this when he publicly declares: "I am
Alpha and Omega, the beginning and the end" (*alpha* and *omega*
are the first and last letters of the Greek alphabet). To have a Savior

who is at both the initiation and at the culmination is to have a Savior who, by divine fiat, has said it all—all that can be said. It is no mistake that Saint John the gospel writer confidently writes, "When all things began, The Word already was. The Word dwelt with God, and what God was, the Word was. The Word was with God at the beginning, and through him all things came to be; no single thing was created without him" (John 1:1–2).

William Stringfellow owns this truth with a captivating and firm embrace. We cannot rely on mere human words to unwrap or unfold the revelation of God Incarnate, which Christmas itself will always reveal at the end of the first Advent. "The entire vocabulary in human usage is temporal. To employ any of it to attempt to elucidate the finale of time is an extraordinary, and incongruous, effort in which words can never mean simply what they say."[1]

> [My] hope, insofar as it is yet given to me to speak of it, is specifically grounded in the New Testament, which exposes the transience of the politics of this world, but which forebears to renounce political involvement, and which believes the sovereignty of God during this passing age. Simultaneously, the biblical witness anticipates, with extraordinary eagerness, and with no less remarkable patience, the end of this world's politics, the perishing of this age, the judgment of the nations and principalities and all rulers, the next advent of Jesus Christ, openly and triumphantly, to vindicate his reign as Lord.[2]

> . . . biblical politics *never* implies a particular, elaborated political theology . . . The gospel is not ideology and categorically, the gospel cannot be ideologized. Biblical politics always has a posture in tension and opposition to the prevalent system . . . Biblical politics are alienated from the politics of this age.[3]

> It is literally pagan, unbiblical, to so recite, "Jesus is the answer." The Bible is more definitive, the biblical

---

1. Stringfellow, *Conscience and Obedience*, 82.
2. Stringfellow, *Conscience and Obedience*, 9.
3. Stringfellow, *Conscience and Obedience*, 12–13.

affirmation is "Jesus is Lord!" The Bible makes a political statement of the reign of Christ preempting all the rulers, and all pretenders to thrones and dominions, subjecting all incumbents and revolutionaries, surpassing the doctrine and promises of the ideologies of this world.[4]

Is it any wonder that magi set out in search of the one "born king of the Jews" (Matthew 2:2)? Is it any wonder that King Herod is seriously threatened by what will occur in a little town called Bethlehem? There is anticipation beyond mere myth or nice story. There is nothing less in our Advent preparation than *Advent itself*. Anticipation that a king has come, is here, and will come again rings throughout the coherent Gospels. Our loyalty is beyond the transient and is founded on the God-made-man, a once-infant named Jesus, who is "the Christ," and who will appear again as he appeared before: King and Lord.

Do I worship an infant in swaddling clothes only; do I give homage to an infant who is no threat to me; do I satisfy myself with candlelight and soft music? If I do, good Lord deliver me during this Advent to worship the King, and no other: not even a Christmas image of who he is; who you are. Amen!

---

4. Stringfellow, *Conscience and Obedience*, 13.

TUESDAY

Blessing

The people who walked in darkness, have seen a great light: light has dawned upon them, dwellers in a land as dark as death. Thou hast increased their joy and given them great gladness; they rejoice in thy presence as men rejoice at harvest, or as they are glad when they share out the spoil; for thou hast shattered the yoke that burdened them, the collar that lay heavy on their shoulders, the driver's goad, as in the day of Midian's defeat. All the boots of trampling soldiers and the garments fouled with blood shall become a burning mass, fuel for fire. For a boy has been born for us, a son given to us, to bear the symbol of domination on his shoulder; and he shall be called in purpose wonderful, in battle God-like, Father for all time, Prince of Peace. (Isaiah 9:2–6)

The blessings promised to Israel in this Isaiah passage apply to all God's people, for Jesus is born to humankind. Whether prince or pauper, one can expect this one "born for us" and "given to us" is prophecy and promise for all. Israel's Messiah would become the Savior of the world.

Stringfellow himself worked in Harlem, New York City for many years, advocating for the poor and oppressed of that area of the city. Such legal ministry, done pro bono, was done with String-fellow living among those he served. The Babylonian captivity of Israel seemed to have a firm grip on the Harlem parish of Stringfellow's assignment.

> . . . there were other fronts which required attention besides the politics of the city and the practice of law in Harlem. I had come initially to Harlem as a member of the group ministry of the East Harlem Protestant Parish, out of concern for the missions of the Church to the poor and to those socially discriminated against in the city.
>
> When I first moved to the neighborhood the parish was suffering from a terrific confusion as to the nature of the church and of the meaning and manner of the Church's task in a place such as Harlem. At the heart of these issues were some of the same matters which so divide the several churches outside of Harlem. They provoked deep divisions within the parish, particularly among the members of the group ministry, who, apart from myself and one other man, were clergymen.
>
> Through its first years in the neighborhood the parish had become deeply conformed to the world. Conformity to the world is a temptation which assails the Church no less in the slums than in the suburbs. Conformity to the world exists whenever and wherever the Church regards its message and mission to be primarily determined by, or essentially dominated by, the ethos of secular life and the society which surrounds the Church.
>
> The young ministers who had come out of Union Theological Seminary to found the East Harlem Protestant Parish were much tempted by such conformity. They had seen the Protestant churches abandon the inner city, both physically and psychologically, and were aroused by this attachment and conformity of Protestantism to middle-class American society. They would bring the ministry of Protestantism back into the inner city and work there among the poor and the dispossessed. In doing so they were confronted with how the ministry could be exercised in the midst of the long-festering, complex, and to them—since they were white middle- and upper-class people—unfamiliar social problems that

characterize urban slum society. To these problems they brought two things—a hostility toward the conventional churches outside the slums, which caused them to think they had little or nothing to learn from the Church outside East Harlem, and a sincere passion for social change and revolution, even, in East Harlem. These two emotions joined to underscore the view that before the Gospel could be preached and received by the people in the slums, the way for the Word had to be prepared by improving the education of the people, renovating their housing, finding jobs for them, clearing the streets of garbage and debris, challenging the political status quo, alleviating the narcotics problem, and by social action of all sorts. When some of these issues had been resolved, when the lives of the people were less burdened with poverty, discrimination, illiteracy, and ignorance, then the time would come to preach the Gospel and then the people, no longer preoccupied with their afflictions, would be able to hear and embrace the Gospel.[1]

The promise of the first Advent is not that all will be made right and then Messiah will appear on the world's stage. Instead, just when Israel and the nations were at their lowest, when Israel had sensed it was still held in captivity and a new exodus was necessary, before the revolution, the gospel would appear. Prophetic truths record the words of hope in the midst of hopelessness and joy in the presence of lament.

Lord, keep me from fearing and fretting the darkness as if you cannot do your work when there seems to be no light. Remind me that we need not make over anything—that you indeed make everything over; you make everything new. Anything I have to bring to the equation is really nothing at all. Make me know that nothing that preoccupies me can stand in the way of the gospel, and I will be at peace. Amen!

1. Stringfellow, *My People Is the Enemy*, 85–86.

WEDNESDAY

Christ(ianity)

There is no salvation in anyone else at all, for there is no other name under heaven granted to men, by which we may receive salvation. (Acts 4:12)

If we are speaking of soul sleep, Nirvana, "oneness" with the universe, in the same conversation with the concept of salvation as revealed in the Word of God and as understood by Christians *historically*, we may have the question of religious ends as a subset of the study of world religions. But once we push down on the truth of salvation we encounter parameters which define us and our chosen theme, Christianity, as a unique salvation. Stringfellow thought American Christians particularly at risk at this point.

> Sometimes, somewhat paradoxically, this idea [that "being sincere" is enough in religion] is coupled with praise of the religious origins of American society, the common talk of Americans as a deeply religious people, and reference to vague spiritual values to which the nation is just as vaguely committed. Such an instance took place during the 1960 presidential campaign when Mr. Nixon indicated that though, of course, religion should not influence politics, the American people were after all an essentially religious folk who would not care to elect

a President who had no religion. One must have some religion, though it doesn't really matter what it is.

Religion, in such a view, becomes a wholly subjective thing, looking for its content, if it has any, to the imagination, intelligence, innovation of the believer. Consequently, religion, in this sense, is an utterly erratic thing, the content of which changes from one time to another and from what one man says to what another man says. Religion, then, becomes, indeed all things to all men simultaneously.

But to imply that all religion is the same, that all religion is completely contingent upon the one who believes, is tantamount to atheism. It is quite the same thing as saying that there is no God—at least no God who may be known, no living God; that there is no historically active God who has his own presence, apart from whether or not his presence is acknowledged; no God who has His own integrity, apart from minds or feelings of men; no God has His own identity, apart from the existence of men; no God whose mode of action is consistent and faithful and ubiquitous in the world and which may be beheld and to which men may respond in one way or another. The man who declares that it makes no difference what you believe so long as you believe something is declaring that there is no truth, that there is no ultimate meaning which has immediate and concrete significance for the world, that there is no God.

Christians, at least in Protestantism in America, have been intimidated far too long by this idea. It is argued that this is the American conception, one which safeguards the religious freedom and that it is anyway pragmatically essential to harmony among the diverse religious groups in society. The argument wears thin, however, in the face of the experience of other democratic societies—Britain and Scandinavia and Western Europe—where the public freedom to practice religions of various kinds appears not to be abridged by the existence of established churches. If this doctrine is, in fact, a safeguard for the public freedom of religious practice, it is at least not the only one imaginable or available within the democratic tradition. And at what price is this alleged harmony accomplished if in fact the doctrine upon which it rests requires a religious folk a profession, in effect, of atheism?

Insofar as American Protestantism begins now, in the ecumenical discussions with Roman Catholic and Orthodox and Anglican Christians, to remember something of the corporate existence of the Church, something of the Oneness and Holiness of the Body of Christ, it must necessarily and inevitably abandon its historic association-it's guilty association-with the radical individualism which has so dominated its thought and organization and way of life in the United States. The auspices which Protestantism has provided for the notions that all religion is the same, and that each individual is an authoritative arbiter of religious truth, have inhibited evangelism in the name of the Church, have jeopardized prophetic witness, and have gravely corrupted the corporate worship of Christians. Moreover, the accommodation of Protestantism to these American religious notions has impaired the responsibility of the Protestant churches to undertake any critical stance in religion to the nation and to American society . . .

Christians cannot be parties to a truce founded upon the assertion that it matters not what a man believes; rather, they must refute that sort of atheism with the boldness and scandal of their faith in Jesus Christ.[1]

In Jesus Christ, there is no chasm between God and the world.

Jesus Christ means that God cares extremely, decisively, inclusively, immediately for the ordinary, transient, proud, wonderful, besetting, profane, frivolous, heroic, lusty things of men. The reconciliation of God and the world in Jesus Christ means that in Christ there is a radical and integral relationship of all men and of all things. *"In Him all things are held together."*[2]

Deliver me, Lord Christ, from diluting my Christianity in a falsely, cowardly move to not offend those of other faiths. Make me

1. Stringfellow, *Private and Public Faith*, 30–32.
2. Stringfellow, *Private and Public Faith*, 40 (Colossians 1:17b).

ready for scandal if it comes but, nonetheless, make me bold no matter what; and with my boldness keep my witness winsome to win some. Amen!

THURSDAY

Death

. . . every day I die . . . (1 Corinthians 15:31)

For through the Law I died to the Law—to live for God. I have been crucified with Christ; the life I now live is not my life, but the life which Christ lives in me . . . (Galatians 2:20)

If we are to speak of the incarnate life of Jesus Christ and the new life that is extended to us through him, we must also speak of his death, our death, and the fact that death is an enemy, but a defeated enemy which, though it will eventually be placed where it belongs, still manifests vestigial remains until the second coming. "For he is destined to reign until God has put all enemies under his feet; and the last enemy to be abolished is death" (1 Corinthians 15:25).

> Having already died in Christ, his [speaking of Anthony, his housemate and soulmate for many years] selfhood had been rescued, established, identified, fulfilled, and finished, so that his death, while poignant, was not waste or tragedy or demonic triumph or incentive for despair. In traditional syntax, Anthony had found his life in his loss of life in Christ . . . We were much aware of how

the efficacy of the resurrection for living here and now impinges among many other ways, upon dying.[1]

"Theologically speaking, what I am talking about is the meaning of the death of Christ that emancipates a human being from bondage to death."[2]

By becoming human, Christ Jesus of Nazareth places himself within the temporal time space continuum, and knows, as he grows, that the order of God's ends is life after death after life. Death was in his future. Mary, his mother, was even the recipient of Simeon's prophecy concerning his death when Simeon spoke to Mary, "This child is destined to be a sign which men reject; and you, too, shall be pierced to the heart" (Luke 2:34–35).

> These are issues that have only *historic* answers; that is, the 'answers' of actual events and experiences . . . That assessment literally awaits the prerogatives of the judgment of the Word of God as the consummation of all history. As to that judgment, no person and no principality—least of all the professed church—has insight. The specificity of the judgment of the Word of God endures as mystery until the end and fulfillment of the era of time. And as Saint Paul was mindful, every effort to second-guess the judgment of the Word of God is, for humans or for institutions, a dissipation.[3]

Stringfellow, in many places, tells of the quiet or even silent places he sought for thought and for writing. He and his partner "in community"[4] found great significance to what they had labelled "The Workshop," a small studio toward the rear of their property on Block Island, Rhode Island. Stringfellow writes after Anthony's death, "The Workshop . . . became for him—at the prime of his talent—a way to share who he was and what he knew as a human

---

1. Stringfellow, *Simplicity of Faith*, 39.
2. Stringfellow, *Simplicity of Faith*, 39.
3. Stringfellow, *Simplicity of Faith*, 44.
4. Stringfellow, *Simplicity of Faith*, 48.

being with the rest of the world, or at least with some people who valued their own humanity enough to aspire to be civil!"[5]

> . . . it is exactly to the giving over of all men and all creation and all of creation to the power of death, to which the Christian faith is addressed. Christians confess that the whole burden of human existence in all of its variety is death, and insist that the stark, relentless activity of death in all the works of men—even the works which men imagine to be good—must be confronted, not ignored. Indeed, Christians see that death is the substance and outcome of the estrangement of men from God, and within that, of the separations among men and of the hostility between men and the rest of creation . . .

> It is, instead, the knowledge that there is no pain or privation, no humiliation or disaster, no scourge or distress or destitution or hunger, no striving or temptation, no wile or sickness or sufferings or poverty which God has not known or borne for men in Jesus Christ. He has borne death itself on behalf of men, and in that event, He has broken the power of death once and for all.[6]

I, as did the apostle Paul, "reckon, count, consider" myself dead indeed in Christ. No matter what the temptation, I pray I be aided never to take up my own, my old life up again—by your Holy Spirit, show me the life before death before life, is your method to bring about my bowing the knee to the Word of God. Amen!

---

5. Stringfellow, *Simplicity of Faith*, 51.

6. Stringfellow, *My People Is the Enemy*, 31–32.

FRIDAY

Emmanuel

Therefore, the Lord himself will give you a sign: a young woman will be with child, and will bear a son, and will call him name Emmanuel. (Isaiah 7:14)

The word *Emmanuel* literally means "God with us" or "God is with us." It is an expression of the relationship of God in his incarnate reality with humanity. It literally means "God in the flesh," or more closely, "in the meat," as in chili con carne. Therefore, the name Emmanuel parallels, or is synonymous with, Stringfellow's use of the phrase *Word of God*. "I intend this to be understood as a name. Thereby I refer not only to the Bible as the Word of God, but simultaneously, to the Word of God, incarnate in Jesus Christ, and, also, to the Word of God militant in the life of the world, as the Holy Spirit, and further, to the Word of God inhering in the whole of creation."[1]

". . . intimacy with the Word of God in the Bible, reliance upon the Word of God in the Bible, is a characteristic of the ordinary practice of the Christian life."[2] Stringfellow cautioned against what he called "a fundamental misapprehension about what the

1. Stringfellow, *Conscience and Obedience*, 14.
2. Stringfellow, *My People Is the Enemy*, 92.

Bible is."[3] It is the revelatory place where we are introduced to the *living* Word of God, Emmanuel. God is intimately found in these "ordinary" practices of life.

The incarnation, leading to the name Emmanuel, gives the Christian a certain perspective, or point of view.

> From the point of view of the Christian faith, the monstrous American heresy is to think that the whole saga of history takes place merely between a celestial God and terrestrial men. But the truth is quite otherwise, both biblically and empirically: The drama of history takes place among God, men, *and* the principalities and powers, those dominant institutions and ideologies active in this world. It is a shallow humanism which encourages Christians to believe that men are masters of these principalities and powers, including racism. In fact, however, racism has been and still remains for both white men and black men in America the reigning idol which replaces God, and represents that power in the world which is superior to all other powers, save God Himself—the power of death.
>
> This is the power with which Jesus Christ was confronted throughout his own ministry and which—at great and sufficient cost—he overcame. This is the power with which any man who is a Christian has contended and from which—by his own participation in the death in Christ—he is set free. This is the power which must be exposed and openly confronted if there is to be true reconciliation and not simply a modest degree of secular integration in America.
>
> The issue, at least for Christians—though in the end for every man—is what it means *to be a man.* Much more is involved that legal equality. Much more is at stake than common morality, natural law, or democratic axioms . . . More—and something different—is required than improved education, better job opportunities, and public integration, if a man is to be a man.
>
> What it means to be a man is to be free from idolatry in any form, including, but not alone, idolatry of race.

3. Stringfellow, *My People Is the Enemy*, 93.

What it means to be a man is to know that all idolatries are tributes to death, and then to live in freedom from all idolatries. To be a man means to be freed from the worship of death by God's own affirmation of one's own life in Christ. To be a man means the freedom, in the first place, to love yourself in the way in which God Himself has shown that He loves every man . . .

Into that freedom, from time to time, men are baptized. In that freedom men are born into the society of all mankind wrought by God in the life and ministry of Christ. In that freedom is the way and witness of the Cross in which is reconciliation. In that freedom is the love and unity among men which can endure death for the sake of all, even unto a man's own enemy, even unto my own enemy, even unto myself.[4]

Lord, aid my prayers to reflect more and more the reality of the "life and ministry of Christ," your Emmanuel. Help me to anticipate the immensity of God's, of your being "with us" as a fact of history and a reality of common, everyday life. May I expect you to always be with us—and to be with me, when I least feel it and need to know it. Amen!

---

4. Stringfellow, *My People Is the Enemy*, 147–49.

SATURDAY

Freedom

Let us then stop discussing the rudiments of Christianity. We ought not to be laying over again the foundation of faith in God and of repentance from the deadness of our former ways, by instruction about cleansing rites and the laying-on-of-hands, about the resurrection of the dead, and eternal judgment. Instead, let us advance toward maturity; and so we shall if God permits. (Hebrews 6:1–3)

The freedom of God in his ruling love for this world in this world is not at all coincident with, contingent upon, nor captive of the Church, much less so of the churches or of individual Christians. If the Church or those within the churches do not see and honor the freedom of God, if they will not thus acknowledge and worship God, if they persist in vain commendations of themselves instead of in gladness in the Word of God, if they indulge in boasting witness to themselves rather than bragging of their weakness to explain and attest God's grace and strength, if they conceive of salvation as in part attributable to themselves and not wholly the gift of God's initiative in this world, then God, as has been the case before, in his terrible and magnificent generosity with himself in the world, will simply find his own way of working his will and do without the churchly institutions and those who profess to be Christians and, so to speak, take over wholly himself the ministry of the Church.

This has, after all, happened before, as the Letter to the Hebrews so forcibly reminds. The Word of God was not absent from the history of this world before the birth of Jesus Christ. In fact and by the biblical testimony creation itself and all that is therein is given life in the utterance of that same Word disclosed in Jesus Christ. The Word of God is delivered in various ways in diverse times in the history of the world, and in the gift of the Word within history a people of the Word, a peculiar nation, Israel, is called into being.

But the day comes to pass—long foreshadowed in the Prophets and in the Psalms; and later premonitive in the birth and earthly ministry of Jesus Christ, in the hostility of the worldly rulers to Christ, and his rejection at the hands of his own people and disciples, in his absolute abandonment—when Jesus Christ is, on the Cross, the embodiment within himself of God's people. The day, Good Friday, comes when Christ *is* Israel and there is no Israel as an authentic people of God save the remembrance, presence, and pioneer of that people in Christ himself. God, then and there, simply accepts the fact that he had been renounced and deserted by his own people, just as he was left by Adam, and perseveres in his own witness to himself as God which is his work of salvation.

In his time, by his own witness, according to his own will, by the generosity of his Godliness, in his compassion and forgiveness, in his freedom as God, God establishes in the aftermath of the resurrection of Christ, at Pentecost, a New Israel, the Church. This is the Body of Christ into which God elects all those who believe in him, that is, all those who beseech and trust the Word of God overwhelming the power of death in their own lives and in all the world.

But make no mistake about this: that God in the intercession of Christ in the world assembles and unites and ratifies a new nation, the Church, for himself and for his world does not mean that the same Church is thereby immune from the temptations of death, the wiles of the devil, the vanities common to all men, the substitution of idols for God, the glorification of self, forsaking the faith, apostasy, skepticism, heresy, and unbelief. God gives the Church sufficient freedom to resist, refute, and renounce all of these things, but God's grace is not so cheap, unloving, and mechanistic as to shield the Church or its members from suffering the assaults of all these things.

In short, the new one holy nation, the Church, which inherits the Cross of Christ, shares the gift of the Holy Spirit, and succeeds to the old nation, Israel, which had abdicated to death and advocated the Cross for Christ, is vulnerable to this day to every attack and tactic within the range and service of the power of death. And if, under such aggression, the Church as Church does not survive, even as Israel, then it may confidently be expected of God's mercy that he will again assume the task of the Church and witness to himself, just as God in Christ assumed the whole witness of Israel to God on the Cross.

The freedom of God in this world in his witness to himself is never mitigated, confounded, delayed, or precluded by the compromise of the integrity of the Church as his witness by the Church, by the churches, or among members of the Church. What is at stake may be the very existence of the Church as a people, or of a particular Church body, or of a member of the Church, but what is never at stake is the efficacy of God's own witness to himself and, within that, to the given and true life of the whole world in reconciliation. What is at stake is not whether there will be an ample witness to the Word of God, but whether those who call themselves Christian and those who use the name of the Church will be deprived of the pleasure and prerogative of participating in God's witness to himself in this history.[1]

Keep me always from disqualifying myself as a witness to the Incarnate Christ and the work of God within his freedom to work in each of his people, in the local church, and in the Church. Don't allow me to place myself on a shelf where I may exist in isolation, needing

1. Stringfellow, *Free in Obedience*, 107–10.

freedom. Set me free within the freedom which is yours alone, and I will be "free indeed." Amen!

WEEK II

SUNDAY

If any of you falls short in wisdom, he should ask God for it and it will be given him, for God is a generous giver who neither refuses nor reproaches anyone. (Hebrews 1:5)

Wisdom means knowledge of God. Wisdom is the knowledge of God given to men in this world which embraces all other knowledge within the limits of human awareness and comprehension, particularly the profound knowledge of self in relationship to all men and all things in this world.

Knowledge as Gift: The knowledge of God in which the truth of all existence inheres is an authentic gift and not something earned through diligence or piety, or rewarded for sacrifices of any description, or dependent upon any human initiative, or contingent upon the beliefs of men. It is a *gift,* and as with any genuine gift it originates wholly in the disposition of the donor and is accomplished entirely by the voluntary action of the donor. A gift can be refused or dishonored, one can vainly imagine himself deserving of a gift, a gift can be squandered or misconstrued, one may despise or be threatened by the generosity of the giver, but no responses such as these in any way negate the event of the gift, impair its value, or impeach the donor.

It is thus when one person makes a gift to another; it is no less so when a gift is made by God.

In American society, integrity in giving is rare. Giving has come to designate all sorts of transactions that bear little resemblance to gifts. People "give" out of a sense of obligation; they describe exchanges of chattels as "gifts"; they contribute to charities to purchase a sense of satisfaction; they "give" presents to one another in almost automatic reaction to commercial stimuli; they observe days and seasons with ritual "giving." Such vulgarities are no gifts. The real gift is always voluntary, spontaneous, free of expectancy either of equivalent return or gain of any kind, and representative of the giver. Actually the only thing that can be given by a person to another is himself. Any authentic gift is a means by which one offers to another knowledge of himself in a way that affirms the identity of the recipient as well as declares who the donor is. A gift is a sacrament of existence in a relationship established by the initiative of the giver. The prerogative in the relationship belongs wholly to that act of giving. No one can really know me unless I give him such knowledge. I cannot truly know another unless he gives that knowledge to me.

The wisdom that constitutes knowledge of God and within that, all knowledge, is verily a gift, given to men by God in this world. Jesus Christ is the epitome of that gift. This does not mean that men in this world are bereft of knowledge of God apart from Christ, for knowledge of God is given in all created things; rather, it means that all that is known of God in this world is embraced, verified, and consummated in Jesus Christ. In Jesus Christ all that men may know in this world of God is made known. It is not beyond God's mercy that there is more to know of him than that given to men in this world to know, but it is the measure of God's love for this world that no more is known of him than that which is known through Jesus Christ.

God is neither shy nor modest in giving knowledge of himself to men, for this gift is given to all men whether a man welcomes or ignores it. From no man is this gift withheld despite even the power of sin. The gift is offered in the first instance, as it were, in the event of Creation itself; but the gift is renewed in the Fall. No matter how terrible the emptiness men endure within themselves and the alienation men suffer from all other men and all things in their estrangement from God, that does not blot out the gift. Or, to put it in the images of Genesis, after the Fall, in the depth's of man's emphatic rejection of God and pathetic negation of man's own life, the first characterization of God's response to rejection is of God walking in the garden calling to man. "Where are you?" (Genesis 3:8–9). In sin men hide from God and conceal themselves, from one another and fear even to behold themselves; but, in the midst of that, God is seeking men.

That God's love is indomitable, that God perseveres in being available to men, that God reaches out to men though they be sinners, that God's gift of Himself transcends all barriers, attempts to escape, or temptations— all this means that just as God's authorship includes the whole of Creation so also He wills that all of Creation be restored and that all men be saved as His gift. The knowledge of God which is salvation is a gift for *all* men, though every man may not accept the gift and though churchly doctrines may try to hamstring God's grace with religious indulgences. God gives generously and without reproaching (James 1:5b).[1]

Keep me, Lord Jesus Christ, through this Advent and always, from thinking wisdom is something other than the knowledge of you; protect me from the world's lies in tying other characteristics to the term "wisdom." Allow me the peaceable knowledge of yourself which the angels announced at the first Advent: "Glory to God in highest heaven, and on earth his peace for men on whom his favor rests" (Luke 2:14). Amen!

---

1. Stringfellow, *Count It All Joy*, 25–27.

Gift

Remember where you stand not before the palpable, blazing fire of Sinai, with the darkness, gloom, and whirlwind, the trumpet-blast and the oracular voice, which they heard, and begged to hear no more; for they could not bear the command. "If even an animal touches the mountain, it must be stoned." So appalling was the sight, that Moses said, "I shudder with fear."

No, you stand before Mount Zion and the city of the living God, heavenly Jerusalem, before myriads of angels, the full concourse and assembly of the first-born citizens of heaven, and God the judge of all, and the spirits of good men made perfect, and Jesus the mediator of the new covenant, whose sprinkled blood has better things to tell than the blood of Abel. See that you do not refuse to hear the voice that speaks. (Hebrews 12:18–24)

The problem which has always and will always plague the Church and its members is the very problem of the Hebrews, not only before the ministry of Christ, but during his earthly ministry, and, as the Letter to the Hebrews shows, even after his resurrection. The problem is, simply, that of receiving the gift of the Word of God which is salvation from death itself and then, in one fashion or another, concealing from the world this gift which is first entrusted to the Church at Pentecost and to the Christian in baptism. The temptation before the Church and thence before the churches and Christians, is to receive and then covet rather than proclaim and share his gift. The peril is that the gift is disclosed to the world only on condition that the world admire the trustee of the gift rather than the Giver. The world is then profoundly misled and considers the gift as other than what it is.

One example of that is where the Church tries to confine the gospel to standards of conformity and behavior or belief set up by the Church for some sects of the Church. Thus, in the first Israel, the people of God received the gift of the Word of God in the commandments delivered through Moses. The people heard, for instance, in that specific revelation of God's word, that 'thou shalt not kill.' They therefore engaged in defining and limiting the acts and omissions which constitute killing in order to dispense to themselves and promise to other men a means of easy obedience and apparent fidelity to the Word of God.

What actually results is a restriction and alteration of the Word of God into something so soft or simplistic that most men can literally obey the commandment and thus justify themselves without any need of God's grace as judgment or forgiveness. Thus, killing is reduced to certain definitions of actual homicide resulting in death by intentional or negligent violence of the person or persons. But overlooked in such a tempering with God's word are all the meanings of killing beyond the conventional forms of murder and manslaughter which are contained and enacted in our ordinary alienation from one another in, as Christ himself reminds in the Sermon on the Mount, the mere anger of one towards another.

In the Sermon when Christ explicitly discusses the old law, he is not adding to or altering the dimensions of the Word of God disclosed therein; He is rather recalling for Israel the original dimensions of the commandments. He is restoring the truth of the Word in the commandments and exposing how much the Word had been distorted and restricted after its revelation through Moses.

Who is there, after all, among men who has not killed in one way or another and does not fall, therefore, within the judgment Word of God? Who is there who does not need God's mercy, even though he does not want it or would prefer to earn his own salvation? Whenever you regard another human being as less than yourself, you convict yourself of killing him. Whenever a parent exploits an offspring by imposing his or her own personality or aspirations upon the child, murder is done. Whenever sex is primitive aggrandizement of one by another, someone is killed. Whenever a man dishonors his own God-given life by anger, greed, hate, envy, insult, or malice, he takes his own life no less than a suicide. All men are not murderers in the sense of violent, negligent, or passionate deadly assault on another's life, but no man is innocent of violating the commandment of the Word of God not to kill.

Such a radical and inclusive scope applies as well to the other commandments. As a result, there is no man who is not liable judgment, and there is none without need of forgiveness. This is just as true of men today as it was to the Israelites who listened to Moses or to the hearers of the Sermon on the Mount.

The Word of God is belittled when in the Church or in one of the churches the Word is construed in a fashion that makes obedience to the Word of God not dependence upon grace but a convenient moralistic, pietistic, or ritualistic conformity. Some of the common examples in American churches of such conformity do not have the dignity of an even tolerable biblical basis. That is the case with those sects which teach that the practice of the Christian life chiefly consists of abstention from smoking, drinking, and dancing; those which make a fetish about customs of diet and dress; those which regard attendance and churchly rites and ceremonies magically or mechanistically; or those which disregard the wholeness of the Bible and select from it the fragments which seem to reinforce and condone what they prefer to say and do. None of these practices has any inherent efficacy to save a man from the power of death, nor will any of them enable a man to escape the fullness of God's judgment. And all such efforts only imitate the disrespect shown for the Word of God in the earlier days of the old Israel.[1]

[Yet] . . . in almost any congregation of virtually any denomination, one will find and can expect to find some Christian people who take seriously the authority of their baptism and live and work within the churches and in the world as emissaries of the Kingdom already present in the world which is the Church of Christ.[2]

When you look upon the landscape of your creation and the witness of the Word of God within it, I ask that I be found distributing the gift received rather than hoarding it in selfish egoism. Deliver me from ever thinking that what you give is mine alone. Christ for the world—let this my motto be. Amen!

---

1. Stringfellow, *Free in Obedience*, 110–112.
2. Stringfellow, *Free in Obedience*, 106.

TUESDAY

Holy Spirit

The angel said to her, "The Holy Spirit will come upon you, and the power of the Most High will overshadow you; and for that reason the holy child to be born will be called 'The Son of God.'" (Luke 1:34–35)

Spirituality is for many, particularly church folk, an intimidating term. It is recited authoritatively yet merely conceals a void . . .

> This whole matter of the elusive significance of so-called spirituality comes into acute focus, for me, in the cursory and profane regard which the name of the Word of God as the Holy Spirit suffers, more often than not, within the churches. I remember, for instance, that I was very impatient to be confirmed in the Episcopal Church. In my rearing as a child in that church I had come to think that confirmation was the occasion when the secrets were told. Confirmation, I supposed, was the event in which all the answers that had been previously withheld from me, because I was a child, would be forthcoming. In particular, I recall, I was eager to be confirmed because I expected in confirmation to learn the secret of the Holy Spirit. At last, I anticipated, my curiosity concerning this mysterious name would be satisfied.

In my experience as a child, in the church, when adults named the Holy Spirit in the presence of children it was always an utterly obscure, unspecified, literally spooky allusion.

It did not specifically occur to me as a child to suspect that adults in the church did not know what they were talking about when they used the name of the Holy Spirit. The reference, anyway, was always intimidating. The mere invocation of the name, without any definition, connection, or elaboration, would be effective in aborting any issues raised by a child. "The Holy Spirit" was the great, available, handy stopper.

Needless to say, confirmation turned out to be a great disappointment to me . . . if anything, the name of the Holy Spirit was put to use in confirmation instruction with even deeper vagueness . . .

After I had begun to read the Bible seriously, on my own initiative . . . the cloture about the Holy Spirit was disrupted and the ridiculous mystification attending of *this* name of the Word of God began to be dispelled. In contrast to my childish impressions from experiences in church, I found the Bible to be definitive and lucid as to the identity, character, style, and habitat of the Holy Spirit. In the Bible, the Holy Spirit is no term summoned simply to fill a void, or to enthrall rather than instruct the laity, or to achieve some verbal sleight-of-hand because comprehension is lacking. Biblically, the Holy Spirit names the faithfulness of God to his own creation. Biblically, the Holy Spirit means the militant presence of the Word of God inhering in the life of the whole of creation. Biblically, the Holy Spirit is the Word of God at work both historically and existentially, acting incessantly and pervasively to renew the integrity of life in this world. By virtue of this redundant affirmation of the biblical witness, the false notion—nourished in my childhood in the Episcopal Church—that the Holy Spirit is, somehow, possessed by and enshrined within the sanctuary of the church was at last refuted, and I was freed from it. Coincidentally, as one would expect, the celebration in the sanctuary became, for me, authentic—a eucharist for the redemption of the life of the whole of creation in the Word of God—instead of vain ritual or hocus-pocus.

It was the biblical insight into the truth of the Holy Spirit that signaled my own emancipation from religiosity. It was the biblical news of the Holy Spirit that began, then, to prompt the expectancy of encounter with the Word of God in any and all events in the common life of the world and in my own life as part of that. It was—it is—the biblical saga of the Word of God as Agitator, as the Holy Spirit, that assures me that wheresoever human conscience is alive and active, *that* is a sign of the saving vitality of the Word of God in history, here and now.[1]

Holy Spirit, deliver me from vague, "comforting" hopes of you into understanding that you are the goading presence of the Word of God to keep me moving in the redemptive direction which is your will. Your presence assures that I am not stagnant—not left alone to my own devices. Amen!

1. Stringfellow, *Politics of Spirituality*, 16–18.

WEDNESDAY

Incarnation

When all things began, the Word already was. The Word dwelt with God and what God was, the Word was. The Word, then, was with God at the beginning, and through him all things came to be . . . So, the Word became flesh; he came to dwell among us and we saw his glory, such glory as befits the Father's only Son, full of grace and truth. (John 1:1–2, 14)

For the divine nature was his from the first; yet he did not think to snatch equality with God, but made himself nothing, assuming the nature of a slave. Bearing the human likeness, revealed in human shape, he humbled himself, and in obedience accepted even death— death on a cross. (Philippians 2:6–8)

. . . the most elementary characterization of the Gospel of Jesus Christ is the Incarnation. The Incarnation is not a theological abstraction—though it is often presented that way in catechism. It is not some quaint or spooky figure of speech. It is not even a difficult mystery; on the contrary, the Incarnation means that God Himself, in Christ, has shattered for men the very mystery of His being and purpose and activity in this world. The Incarnation means that God's passion for the world's actual life—including its politics, along with all else—is such that He enters and acts in this world for himself. Apart from the Incarnation there is no meaning in the Christmas message that God is with men, nor in the Easter assurance that God acts in this world for the benefit of all men, nor in the Pentecost evidence that God inaugurates the true society which is the Church.

In other words, the Church and Christians are not simply involved in politics because of the nature of politics as such—by which all are involved and abstinence is fiction—but because they honor and celebrate God's own presence and action in the world, because they know that the world—in all its strife and confusion, brokenness, and travail—is the scene of God's work and the subject of God's love.

According to the Gospel, God is not confined to the sanctuaries of the Church. He is not enshrined in any altar. The reason Christians gather now and then in their sanctuaries is not because God is there but rather to celebrate and proclaim God's presence and action outside the sanctuaries in the common life of the world. Worship which has integrity in the Gospel is always an intercession by God's people for the cares and needs of the world, and always a thanksgiving—a eucharist—for God's love for the world. Worship at the altar is thus authenticated by the constant involvement of the people of the Church in the world's life and by the public witness of the Church in the world.

It is sometimes asserted that the Church should concern itself only occasionally in public affairs, where society is confronted with a "moral" issue. The problem with that view is that it oversimplifies the moral conflict in the world. There is no issue in society which is not a moral issue in both the transient human sense and also as one which God judges. In a fallen world, all men live at each other's expense, and every decision and action, even those which seem trivial or only private or unambiguous, is consequentially related to the lives of all men.

What you or I decide and do affects all other men, and every decision or action or omission is thus not only a moral but a theological issue, a sacrament of one's responsibility for and love for one's self and other men, or else a sign of one's disregard for and alienation from one's self and other men. Indeed, on the Last Day, though not before, God's own judgment of every act, word, and deed of every man will expose the true moral disposition of each man in relationship to all men. Meanwhile, each of us must make his own decisions, knowing that each decision is a moral decision with consequences for all other men, but, not knowing what many of those consequences are or will be until he is judged by God's mercy. Meanwhile, each Christian, remembering his Baptism, must take his stand in the practical affairs of this world with fear and trembling . . .

There is no convenient set of rules, no simple blueprint, no simplistic ethics of decision for the Christian. The Christian witness in society does not consist of praising and practicing the "Golden Rule," which, after all, is a secular ethic of self-interest that demeans the essence of the Gospel . . .

Of all men, the Christian is the most blunt and relentless realist. He is free to face the world as it is without flinching, without shock, without fear, without surprise, without embarrassment, without sentimentality, without guile or disguise. He is free to live in the world as it is . . .

That is why the Church of Christ is the only society in this world worthily named great.[1]

Give each of us the "audacity to trust" the love of God for each of us and for the world. Remind us that grace and redeeming action are the mind and action of God—your mind, Lord Christ—your action in the world. Keep us from doctrinaire interpretations of incarnation and allow us to see clearly the truth that God came as human flesh to affirm and to redeem the entire cosmos. Amen!

1. Stringfellow, *Dissenter in a Great Society*, 158–64.

THURSDAY

Joy

Now in the same district there were shepherds in the fields, keeping watch through the night over the flock, when suddenly there stood before them an angel of the Lord, and the splendor of the Lord shone round them. They were terror-stricken, but the angel said, "Do not be afraid; I have good news for you: there is great joy coming to the whole people. Today in the city of David a deliverer has been born to you—the Messiah, the Lord." (Luke 2:8–11)

Therefore, my brothers, I implore you by God's mercy to offer your very selves to him: a living sacrifice, dedicated and fit for his acceptance, the worship offered by mind and heart . . . Let hope keep you joyful; in trouble stand firm; persist in prayer. (Romans 12:1, 12)

At no point in the witness of the Church to the world is its integrity as a reconciled society more radical and more cogent than in the liturgy, the precedent and consummation of that service which the Church of Christ and the members of the Body render to the world . . . there are many . . . who regard the liturgy as peripheral to the Christian life. Some even boast that *they* have no liturgical life, but this is a betrayal of ignorance, since liturgy means nothing more than style of life. In the broadest sense, all of life is liturgical . . .

As for the Church, all forms of its corporate life— from the Quakers sitting in silence in a circle, to the exuberance and patience of a Negro congregation, and the majesty and richness of the venerable Orthodox service—are liturgical. The only serious question is whether or not a given liturgical practice has integrity in the Gospel . . . Some regard liturgy superstitiously, as something with an intrinsic efficacy, as a means of procuring indulgence, as if God were so absurd—and so ungodly—as to be appeased by the redundant incantations of men.

There is, however, nothing so spooky or lucky about the liturgy, and nothing magical or mechanistic about its performance. The liturgy of the Gospel is, on the contrary, a dramatic form of the ethical witness of Christians in this world. In this sense, there may be much variety in different times and cultures in regard to language, music, action, and movement, the liturgy is always characterized by certain definitive marks:

1) *Scriptural Integrity*—The liturgy of the Gospel is the theatricalization of the biblical saga of God's action in this world, thus relating the ubiquity of the Word of God in history to the consummation of the of the Word of God in Jesus Christ. . .

2) *The Historicity of the Liturgy*—The liturgy of the Gospel is both a transcendent event and a present event. It shatters the categories of time and space and location because it both recalls and dramatizes the estate of Creation in the Word of God, and beseeches and foretells the end of history . . .

   Thus the liturgy is the normative and conclusive ethical commitment of the Christian people to the world . . .

3) *The Sacramental Authenticity of the Liturgy*—It is both this transcendence of time in time and the scriptural integrity of the liturgy of the Gospel which constitutes the sacramental essence of the liturgy . . . The liturgy *is* social action because it is

the characteristic style of life for human beings in this world . . .

Baptism bestows the power to live in Christ as a servant of the world . . . For the man who is baptized, the world as it is, is precious. It is the recipient of love because God made it; as the Apostle James reminds us, his Word is to be beheld in all things and in all men. Christians are called to enjoy God's presence in the world for the sake of those in the world who cannot yet do so. While involved in the world, the Christian is characteristically, profoundly, and constantly immersed in the Bible, because it is the testimonial evidence of God's care for, and activity in, this world. From the Bible, we discern, the manner of God's presence and vitality in the world's common life. Christians see the ministry of Jesus Christ as the example of what it is to be reconciled within one's self, with all men and all things in the mercy and judgment of God.[1]

I have consciously plunged myself into the Word of God, the Bible; therefore, Lord Jesus Christ, immerse me with its theme, its action, its demands, its coherence, that through it I will know you better, serve you more willingly, experience you more deeply, and witness to your person and presence more profoundly—and in these realities, keep me humble for your name's sake. Amen!

---

1. Stringfellow, *Dissenter in a Great Society*, 150–56.

FRIDAY

King/Kingdom

Thine, O Lord, is the greatness, the power, and the glory, the splendor and the majesty; for everything in heaven and on earth is thine; thine, O Lord, is the sovereignty, and thou art exalted over all as head. Wealth and honor come from Thee; thou rulest over all; might and power are of thy disposing; thine it is to give power and strength to all. And now, we give thee thanks, our God, and praise thy glorious name. (1 Chronicles 29:12–13)

I conclude that both forecasters and scholastic revisionists misconstrue the meaning of eschatological imminence.

Because time inheres in the reality of death and because the Kingdom destroys death's reign and abolishes time, to think and speak, at all, of the coming of the Kingdom must comprehend the significance of the ending of time. At the outset, it must be realized, thought and speech are taxed because both remain confined in time. The entire vocabulary in human usage is temporal. To employ any of it to attempt to elucidate the finale of time is an extraordinary, and incongruous, effort in which words can never mean simply what they say.

Recognizing that much cautions against any simplistic literalism or any merely historically conditioned interpretation and prays for a more mature and profound communication in which the words, uttered in time, are sacramentalized or transfigured, and that fittingly, since the topic is the Eschaton.

Characteristically, the biblical witness, in Scripture as such and in the life of the church, speaks in marvelously versatile and appropriately diverse ways of the second advent: prophetically, metaphorically, parabolically, ecstatically, sacramentally, dogmatically, poetically, narratively—in every tongue or style or syntax or idiom available. The biblical witness speaks, thus, multifariously of the coming of the King and his kingdom to show that the subject is inexhaustible and one which truly exceeds the capabilities of human speech.

This is an aspect of the sense of imminence biblical people have concerning the Kingdom. More than that imminence expresses eternal reality in time, a way of representing how the eschatological is freed from time, or of bespeaking the ending of time before time has ended. The relationship, in other words, between the Word of God and creation, even in time, transcends time and is, from a human point of view, imminent at any time. In the Word of God a thousand years are not more than a moment.

If some have put aside the expectation, it is not because Christ is tardy and not because God has postponed the next advent, but because the consciousness of imminence has been confused or lost. I regard the situation of contemporary Christians as much the same as that of our early predecessors in the faith so far as anticipation of the Second Coming matters. We expect the event at any moment. We hope for it in every moment. We live in the imminence of the Eschaton. That is the only way, for the time being, to live humanly.

The conviction of eschatological imminence which informs the witness of biblical people during this passing age is grounded in the insight they bear, on behalf of the life of the world, into the political secret of the first advent, which also inheres in creation itself in spite of the fall, that is, the Lordship of Christ. Knowledge of the truth hidden in the first advent, confession of Christ as Lord, means recognition of the sovereignty of the Word of God acting in history to restore dominion to humanity in creation. The anticipation of the second advent is for the consummation of Christ's reign as Lord so that what is secret becomes notorious, what is revealed is transfigured triumphantly, what is witnessed biblically is publicly vindicated.

In the dispensation between (as it were) the two advents, which is no more than a moment for the Word of God or in the expectation of the people of God, the task of Christians is shaped by the imminent, constantly impinging, eschatological hope. And, as I was saying, it is this which becomes crucial in decisions and actions of conscience and obedience in nation and in church, rather than, as is so vainly and persistently supposed, the operation of some great principle. The ethics of biblical people concerns events not moral propositions. And if to the world, to fellow citizens of some nation or to the ruling powers, the way of the biblical witness seems enigmatic, inconsistent, sometimes apparently contradictory, suspect, foolish, then so be it. Christians do not covet anyone's approval or applause, least of all do they seek or envy the sanctions of governments. The Christian life has its only—and its only possible—explication in the judgement of the Word of God.[1]

God, may I, as a biblical person, live with patience for your second Advent, knowing full well that the rule of death which seems so obvious is feigned and judged already. I wish to live in faith and hope, based on your grace, confessing the Word of God in the midst of life here and now. Where I falter, help me I pray. Amen!

---

1. Stringfellow, *Conscience and Obedience*, 82–84.

SATURDAY

Lord/Lordship

For Scripture says, 'As I live, says the Lord, to me every knee shall bow and every tongue acknowledge God.' (Romans 14:11)

. . . I must impress upon you that no one who says, "A curse on Jesus!" can be speaking under the influence of the Spirit of God. And no one can say, "Jesus is Lord!" except under the influence of the Holy Spirit. (1 Corinthians 12:3)

The biblical witness, as the Gospel according to St. John reminds, does not end in the saga of the fall. The biblical testament is completed in Jesus Christ. Jesus Christ means that though the fall ruins creation, the fall does not dissipate the grace of God. Jesus Christ means that though human beings and, indeed, the whole creation reject life as the gift of the Word of God, the Word of God is not thereby retracted or refuted or revoked. Christ means that although in fallen creation vocation is distorted and worship is scandalized, the sovereignty of God is neither disrupted no aborted. Christ means that in the fall, in the midst of the reign of death in time, within the common history of the world, the Word of God nevertheless acts to restore life to the whole of creation. Jesus Christ means that the freedom of God is not curtailed by the fall and not intimidated by the thrall of death, but elects to redeem creation from the power of death. Jesus Christ means the embodiment in human life, now, in this world, of the abundance of the Word of God for salvation from sin and redemption from death for all creation.

Thus it has come to pass that biblical people esteem Jesus Christ as Lord. This is not, as is sometimes erroneously supposed, a title designating the divinity of Christ; it, rather, explicitly explains the humanity of Jesus as the one who epitomizes the restoration of dominion over the rest of creation, vested in human life by the sovereignty of the Word of God during the epoch of the fall. Jesus Christ as Lord signifies the renewed vocation of human life in reconciliation with the rest of creation.

Hence, those who live in Christ and who honor Christ as Lord, are members of the body of the Church of Christ, live in the present age as a "new creation" . . . (2 Cor. 5:17) . . . the essential character of the church in this way has no basic similarity to the ways of human idealism, the practice of religion, or the entertainment of speculations and visions. The claim of the church that it represents in history restored creation is not contingent at all upon virtue in the church but upon the freedom of the Word of God in this world. It is that, I believe, which is the rudimentary and constant cause of tension and friction—the New Testament sometimes refers to *warfare*—between the church and the world, particularly between the church and the nation of the state or other ruling principalities and powers.

At the crux of that incessant conflict is the vocational issue, and, concretely, the discernment which the church, as the exemplar of renewed creation, practices concerning the vocation of political authority. In that witness, the church confesses, on behalf of every nation or state or regime that political authority has a vocation, as every creature does. The church, as it were, remembers that vocation and honors it duly by confessing that political authority is "ordained" or "appointed" by God. Yet, simultaneously, in the midst of the anarchy which is the fall, in this perishing age, while political authority

remains beholden to the powers of death, that confession of the vocation of political authority *always* upholds the preeminence of dominion restored to human life or, in other words, *always* affirms the Lordship of Jesus Christ. But if the church is faithful to Jesus Christ as Lord, can the church ever support political authority in status quo?
. . .

The repudiation of the gift of life and the consignment to the power of death which is the reality of the fall, as has been mentioned, does not avert or abort or estop redemption. The Word of God persists in fallen creation—inherent or residual, hidden or secreted, latent or discreet, mysterious and essential (cf. Rom. 1:20; James 1:21). Having the eyes to behold that presence of the Word, or having the ears to listen to the Word, having the gift of discernment, is, indeed, the most significant way in which Christians are distinguished from other human beings in this world. Yet there is also a sense in which the Word of God, perseverant despite the fall, is attested in the futility of blasphemy; in the impotence of political authority—no matter how beneficent or how beguiling —to achieve the renewal of creation or to approximate the kingdom of God, or, for that matter, to even implement its own mundane ideals and ideologies. It is this confounding of the antiworship indulged by political authority, and by all fallen principalities and powers, which paradoxically confirms the biblical insight that the sovereignty of the Word of God becomes historically notorious in the resurrection of Christ and which inadvertently substantiates the biblical faith that Christ's dominion is triumphant in judgment of political authority and of all creatures and all things whatsoever (Rom. 12:19).[1]

I am convinced that the lordship of Jesus Christ is not a theological talking point or matter of intrareligious argument. Your lordship, Jesus, regardless of my committed affirmation, is biblical and historical fact. For me, it is a matter of my reasoned mind and heart,

---

1. Stringfellow, *Conscience and Obedience*, 31–36.

and I willingly and reverently bow the knee saying, "Jesus Christ is Lord—glory to the Father!" Amen!

WEEK III

SUNDAY

It is by the Holy Spirit that she has conceived this child. She will bear a son; and you shall give him the name Jesus (Savior), for he will save his people from their sins. (Matthew 1:20b–21)

If the name of the Holy Spirit is manipulated or defamed throughout the churches . . . Then it is no wonder that "spirituality" and terms associated with "spirituality," would be recited in disjointed, self-serving, indefinite syntax. Somewhat ironically, there are not only those problems of vagueness and the like with the topic in vocabulary of "spirituality," but also with those occasioned by a veritable plethora of references, allusions, or connections. "Spirituality" may indicate stoic attitudes, occult phenomena, the practice of so-called mind control, yoga discipline, escapist fantasies, interior journeys, and appreciation of Eastern religions, multifarious pietistic exercises, superstitious imaginations, intensive journals, dynamic muscle tension, assorted dietary regimens, meditation, jogging calls, monastic rigors, mortification of the flesh, wilderness sojourns, political resistance, contemplation, abstinence, hospitality, a vocation of poverty, nonviolence, silence, the efforts of prayer, obedience, generosity, exhibiting stigmata, entering solitude, or, I suppose, among these and many other things, squatting on top of the pillar.

The clutter associated with what is called spirituality is accentuated, if not fully or adequately explicated by the frequent and familiar commercial exploitation of both the language and the subject of "spirituality" and, to use an appropriate technical term, the marketing of "spirituality" to mass constituencies inside the boundaries of American Christendom as well as outside those nominal precincts . . . This has rendered "spirituality" vulnerable to commercialization and has caused the yearning of human beings for spiritual integrity in living—as vague or diffuse as such may be—to be articulated in commercialized versions of the crudest degree . . .

The concentration is usually upon self-realization of some sort disconnected with the rest of created life. Where that is the case, however appealing the "spirituality" exemplified may otherwise appear to be, the regime being sponsored or commended is categorically unbiblical. There is no biblical spirituality to be found in a vacuum, cut off from the remainder of humanity within the totality of creation. Indeed, biblical spirituality is significantly about the restoration or renewal of these relationships throughout the realm of created life. To put the same differently, biblical spirituality concerns living in the midst of the era of the Fall, wherein *all* relationships whatsoever have been lost or damaged or diminished or twisted or broken, in a way which is open to transcendence of the fallenness of each and every relationship and in which these very relationships are recovered or rendered new. This transfiguration wrought in biblical spirituality includes one's relationship with oneself, in the most self-conscious and radically personal sense, but it *simultaneously* implicates one concretely in reconciliation with the rest of creation and is thus *the most profoundly political reality available to human experience.* From a biblical perspective, therefore, the assertion of some species of so-called spirituality which is privatized and nonpolitical or anti-political is, simply, nonsense. It is also given the commercialization of much of what is called spirituality a signal to beware of being exploited in more ways than one.

Biblical spirituality represents politics in the broadest possible scope and in a dimension which nurtures, locates, and matures the personal or the self. That is why, I think, the recall of Thomas Merton and his vocation is so lively in so many different places and for so many generations nowadays. It is also one of the reasons why so many alumni—or refugees—from the so-called activism of the decade of the sixties can be beheld today in spiritual pursuits. It is, in part, an endeavor to identify and articulate origins for roots and an effort to comprehend politics within the biblical scenario of creation and fall and redemption.

When all is said and done, however, the aspect of the ambivalence of contemporary "spirituality" that provokes me to be most wary, and has chiefly inhibited the use of such language in my own speaking and writing, is the popular interpretation of "spirituality" as a rejection of the most elementary teaching of the New Testament: the Incarnation. Where the syntax of "spirituality" refers to substance in content at all, and is not just some verbose mishmash, it often represents an emulation of the Greek mentality, or similar pagan attitude, in which the body is separated from the spirit, or the flesh from the soul, or the physical from the spiritual, the material from the mental, the tangible from the ethereal, and so on and on. These dichotomies—unbiblical, false, and basically deceptive—quickly lead to collateral distinctions equally offensive to the gospel of Jesus Christ, like those purporting to distinguish between the profane and sacred, the secular and the sacrosanct, the temporal and the spiritual, the defiled and the pure. Whatever quaintness these juxtapositions may have poetically, theologically they are hostile to the truth of the incarnation. This is, as far as I am concerned, not a matter of doctrine only. Primarily it is an issue of the denial inherent in such supposed dichotomies of the historic event of the implication of the word of God in the common history of this world in Jesus Christ. It is in that event, it is in what has consummately happened in history in Jesus Christ, that all such separations are abolished.

The point is not esoteric but of the immediate practical consequence . . . to commend, thus, the efficacy of the Incarnation.[1]

Your incarnation, Lord Jesus Christ, is so out there when we recite the creed, and so not out there at other times. This cannot be the shortcoming of a priest or pastor, but of me, myself. Put in front of my spiritual life the coherent image of the Incarnate Christ as active in and on and through this present everyday world. Show me my place in his witness. Amen!

1. Stringfellow, *Politics of Spirituality*, 20–22.

MONDAY

Mission

Did you not die with Christ and pass beyond reach of those elemen-
tal spirits of the universe? Then why behave as though you were still
living the life of the world? (Colossians 2:21–22)

"Insofar as [Christianity[1]] in America has not been entrapped in
the religiosity and agnosticism or atheism of religion, the churches
. . . are beset by terrible confusions about the nature of the Church
and the mission of the Church in the world."[2]

Stringfellow, in many ways, paralleled the work of the French
theologian/philosopher Jacques Ellul. They admired one another's
work. In a conversation together, sometime in the late 1950s, Ellul
said "that the dilemma for Christians in France nowadays is this,
that on the one hand, the churches are so debilitated and apostate
that a Christian can hardly bear to remain in the church, and yet,
on the other hand, no Christian can leave a church lest he fail to
confess his own part of the responsibility for the very conditions in
a church which provoked protest."[3]

1. The editor has changed "Protestantism" to "Christianity" insofar as it
applies in 2020, here and where it appears elsewhere in the book.

2. Stringfellow, *Private and Public Faith*, 33.

3. See Ellul, *Presence of the Kingdom*.

At the time Ellul said this, I told him that I did not observe that the situation the churches in the United States was as yet so acute and poignant. But, now, a few years and some second thoughts later, I conclude that Ellul describes the problem here in America as well.

At the same time, a word of caution now needs very much to be added. Within the churches, and, I observed, particularly within the seminaries and among younger clergy, it becomes common to complain caustically and even cynically about the state of the contemporary churches. And while I have not been exactly shy in my own protests, either in my own congregation or in the church at large, and though I am sympathetic to the frustration and disillusionment of the clergy and others, and while I think that there can be no tolerance of the superstitions and out right heresies that in fact much of the lives of the churches and that these must be radically excised—or perhaps more appropriately exorcised—for all that it must be remembered that complaint is not a remedy, and that protest is only the invocation of reform. Let none, in other words, outside the church complain, for only those within the churches know the agony and burden of the disunity, corruption, and weakness of the churches. And let those within the churches act as boldly as they speak lest their reluctance or timidity in acting aggravate further that against which they speak.

Let it be remembered, too, that God does not need the churches. The concern for the purity, fidelity, and unity of the churches as the Church originates in the need of the churches of God, not the other way around. God makes His own witness in the world, and makes that witness even in the very weakness of the churches which are affronts to His name.[4]

Taking a young man to church with him one Sunday morning, Stringfellow recalls the service that day. He writes of the guest preacher:

> . . . upon other occasions I [have] heard him preach the gospel. He did not do so that day. He did not acknowledge

4. Stringfellow, *Private and Public Faith*, 33–34.

Pentecost, nor even, except for an introductory pleas-
antry, the much-celebrated parish anniversary. Instead,
he addressed himself to rather esoteric issue in clergy
politics that had arisen in the diocesan convention a
short time before. It is hard for me to imagine a service,
allegedly the worship God, which would be a more vulgar travesty, though I suppose there are such services. In
any case, my own humiliation for what this must have
conveyed my guest is now much more than it had been
after the earlier service [I had attended].

But it need not have been so. For afterward he knew
that what we had witnessed was neither the proclamation of God's word nor the worship of God, but something more like an alumni rite. And what was wrong with
the preacher was not only that he did not bother with the
Gospel, but that he also did not bother with the people
of the congregation or with their lives and concerns and
problems, whereas my guest knew that real preaching
would be a kind of dialogue between the Word of God
beheld in the Bible and the liturgy, on the one hand,
and on the other, the Word of God as it may be seen
and heard within the common lives of the people of the
congregation.

So my anxiety and wrath and shame were undone.
My friend somehow understood something of the integrity of the Church and the Gospel in seeing and hearing
an event which had little or none of that integrity. In
other words, in every way, in truth but also in pretense,
the Word of God is proclaimed.[5]

And this I relate in order to recall and to caution
myself, as much as any other fond of protest, that as God's
witness cannot be restricted or inhibited by falseness or
weakness in the churches, neither must his witness await
the return of the churches to a better unity and the true
faith.[6]

Cause me to realize that I am coincidental to your witness,
and not constituent of it, Lord Christ. As goes the Church so goes

5. Cf. Philippians 1:18.
6. Stringfellow, *Private and Public Faith*, 35–36.

nothing—for your witness is your own and you are both object and subject. May I see myself as a regular participant in what you are doing in your world and freely then join your mission and not try to create my own. Amen!

TUESDAY

Nation

Seeing then that we have been entrusted with this commission, which we owe entirely to God's mercy, we never lose heart. We have renounced the deeds that men hide for very shame; we neither practice cunning nor distort the word of God; only by declaring the truth openly do we recommend ourselves, and then it is to the common conscience of our fellow men and in the sight of God . . . It is not ourselves that we proclaim; we proclaim Christ Jesus as Lord, and ourselves as your servants, for Jesus' sake. For the same God who said, "Out of darkness let light shine," has caused his light to shine within us, to give the light of revelation—the revelation of the glory of God in the face of Jesus Christ. (2 Corinthians 4:1–2, 5–6)

The precedent of Christian orthodoxy is unchanging, though all else change. Christ is the same yesterday and today and tomorrow. If, in the churches nowadays, the Bible is sometimes read but seldom heard, the Word of God is not muted because the people are deaf. If the historic creeds are recited but not confessed, the precedent is not repealed by such apostasy. If the Gospel is dramatized liturgically, but churchgoers treat this action as simply an empty ritual, the good news is not vitiated because men are superstitious.

Some will complain that the days are too urgent to afford inquiry into the authority in Christian orthodoxy for action in society. When the nation is engulfed in a crisis more momentous than the Civil War, they think there is no time to spend on what they regard as doctrinal niceties. After all, preoccupation with the theological rationalization of action has too often hindered the churches from any active commitment except to their own institutional survival. Did not the fastidiousness of German Christians about theology nourish their apathy toward Nazism?

I have considerable sympathy for such impatience. So much needs to be done if the nation is merely to survive the racial crisis that one must be grateful for those few people who are seriously working for the integration of American society, whether they call themselves Christians or not and however mixed their motivations. Nevertheless, the complaints of the impatient are based on a misconception of orthodoxy, as if it were a pedantic reduction of the Gospel to a propositional scheme which could furnish a basis for application and involvement.

Christian orthodoxy, however, is both historic and existential. It is not to be confused with doctrinal formulations—though these have a certain use and, in a given instance, may be literally true. The substance of Christian orthodoxy, in other words, is no less and none other than the very event of Christ.

Let us put aside all secular legends of Christ and, instructed by 2 Corinthians, no longer count worldly standards important in our understanding of Christ. Let us renounce the well-behaved Jesus innocent of scandal and controversy; the Jesus of superstition memorialized in dashboard statuettes and lucky charms; the fanciful, ineffectual, effeminate, effete Jesus of the cinema whom the multitudes found irresistibly attractive; the soft, spiritual, sentimental Jesus of Salman and other vulgar caricatures; the farsighted Jesus teaching democracy to primitive people centuries before the French and American Revolutions; the imaginary Jesus thought to be an unfortunate victim of a gross violation of due process of law.

Let us, at the same time, forget all religious ideas of Christ; although propagated within the churches, they are only slightly disguised secular notions of him. Let us, in the name of Christian orthodoxy, expose and repudiate the fairy-tale Jesus of Sunday-school story books; the ridiculous Jesus fashioned after the manner of the white Anglo-Saxon Protestant; the unapproachable Jesus captive in tabernacles; the shiny, fragrant Jesus of snow-white raiment unspoiled by sweat or blood or the smell of fish; the religiose Jesus, an ascetic too esoteric for this world.

Let us also leave behind, as St. Paul counsels, the elementary disputes of tradition about the "divinity" of Christ versus the "humanity" of Jesus. This is not so much because they often hide error as because they usually sow confusion; they are not entirely irrelevant, but they encourage dissipation, diverting attention from the actual event of Jesus Christ in this world and thus hindering the actual event of the Christian witness in this world.

Instead, let us behold Jesus Christ as the one whom God has shown Christ to be in this world: the new Adam—the true man—the man reconciled in God.[1]

Grant, oh God, that we behold Jesus Christ as the new Adam— the one who reconciles us and gives to us the ministry of reconciliation—and in the process keep us from thinking for one moment that we have earned, secured, encompassed this reality on our own—in other words, remind us of your grace. May we be a light—or better yet, a reflection of your light to the nations. Amen!

1. Stringfellow, *Dissenter in a Great Society*, 128–30.

WEDNESDAY

Orthodoxy

With this fear of the Lord before our eyes we address our appeal to men. To God our lives lie open, as I hope they lie open to you in your heart of hearts. This is not another attempt to recommend ourselves to you: we are rather giving you a chance to show yourselves proud of us; then you will have something to say to those whose pride is in all outward show and not in inward worth . . . With us therefore worldly standards have ceased to count in our estimate of any man; even if they once counted in our understanding of Christ, they do so, now no longer. When anyone is united to Christ, there is a new world; the old order has passed away, and a new order has already begun. From first to last this has been the work of God. He has reconciled us men to himself through Christ, and he has enlisted us in this service of reconciliation. (2 Corinthians 5:11–13, 16–18)

. . . Let us behold Jesus Christ as the one whom God has shown Christ to be in this world: the new Adam—the true man—the man reconciled in God.

Reconciled *in* God: the preposition helps to emphasize the scope and grandeur of the reconciliation wrought by God in Himself. In the reconciliation in Christ, God and man live as one; encompassed in Him is at once the integrity and wholeness of both God and man, and the unity and love between them and every person and all things. The outreach of the reconciliation which is God's work extends to the whole of creation throughout all places and times. Jesus Christ is the embodiment of that reconciliation. Reconciliation, in terms of Christian orthodoxy, is not some occasional, unilateral, private happening, but, much more than that, the transcendent, universal, and profoundly political event of all time.

Reconciliation is a political event. I realize that, for some, politics is a loathsome word, but, after all, it refers only to the body of interrelationships of men and institutions in this world. Reconciliation is the event, as 2 Corinthians testifies, of a new order of corporate life of men and institutions inaugurated in the world in Christ. In view of this order, it is impossible to consider the reconciliation of one man outside of, or separately from, the estate of all other men and institutions, that is, *politically.* No man speaks truthfully of being reconciled to God who has not suffered reconciliation in God, who is not, in other words, now reconciled with Himself, with all other men, and with all things in the whole of creation.

The event of Jesus Christ, the reconciliation of the whole of creation in time and in the fulness of time, is in behalf of all men; all men benefit from it whether or not they realize it, or desire it, or even like it. It is, simply, the gift of God, acting, as it were, all by Himself among men and in the place of men in this world. It is not something which a man may in any way deserve, purchase, grasp, accomplish, or otherwise procure. As with any gift, it may be opposed, just as Mary resisted Christ's vocation; or it may be refused, just as the multitudes rejected Jesus' ministry; or it may be condemned, just as the ecclesiastical authorities sought to destroy Christ; or it may be dishonored, just as Judas betrayed the Lord; or it may be denied, just as the disciples remained so consistently incredulous until Pentecost, when they endured their own reconciliation with themselves and with the world in God.

All this remains true today. Despite the popularity of heresy within the churches, though men are enthusiastic in their unbelief, even if many men worship their own doubts, and in spite of the public affection for death, nothing avails against the reconciliation of which Christ is the pioneer, the advocate, and the surrogate.

As in earlier times, to be a Christian, a member of Christ's Body, is to be established already, here and now, in this world, in an estate of reconciliation which at once accepts one's self and embraces the whole world. To be a Christian is to receive and know and participate in the unconditional, extravagant, inexhaustible, expendable love of God for all that he has made and called into being. To be reconciled by the virtue of Christ is to be restored to one's own identity in the Word of God, which authorized one's life in the first place, and to be free to identify and affirm the integrity of all other life in that same Word.

To be a Christian, to be already reconciled, means to love the world, all the world, just as it is—*unconditionally.*[1]

Loving the world is so difficult at times; loving others as myself according to Jesus' own command is almost impossible. So grant me, God, by the Holy Spirit, to possess and act on the love which has no human origin but which comes from your own heart. Then, and only then, will I be able to love rightly. Amen!

1. Stringfellow, *Dissenter in a Great Society*, 130–32.

THURSDAY

Preaching

Proclaim the message, press it home on all occasions, convenient or inconvenient, use argument, reproof, and appeal, with all patience that the work of teaching requires. (2 Timothy 4:2)

Stringfellow repeatedly reminds his readers that, against all reasonable contemporary understandings of evangelism, Christians tend to make the church rather than the marketplace the focus. He sees

> . . . the debilitating effect of the abandonment of Biblical preaching and a Biblical liturgy in the congregation upon the service and support of the ministry of the laity and world, and to the significance of confession in the public life and pastoral care of the congregation . . . this is particularly the case with the prophetic ministry of the Church. Even while the preachers (of the churches) have relied with diminishing interest upon the Bible in their preaching, they have often associated the work of preaching with the work of prophetism. Yet, there is no association in principle or historically or functionally between the priest and preacher on the one hand, of the prophet on the other. On the contrary, the former's task is the responsible utterance of the Word of God within

the congregation—so that the Word may be acknowledged and admired there, and so that those who gather as the congregation may be identified by the Word of God in their corporate life as the body of Christ, and so that they may be so enlightened by the Word of God within the congregation that they will become sensitive to and perceptive of the Word of God as they encounter the Word in the common life of the world in which their various ministries as lay people take place. But it is out in the world, not within the congregation, that the prophetic task is exercised. The prophet is characteristically not priest and preacher, but the layman. His task is to represent and expose the Word of God in the world, and particularly in the posture of the Word which stands over against the world's existence and the world's disregard of and arrogance for the Word of God. And sometimes his task is to declare and convey the Word of God as it stands over and against the worldliness of the Church. In either instance, prophetism is not located within the congregation, nor is prophetism particularly associated with preaching in the congregation; rather, prophetism is identified with the clash between the existence of the world and the presence of the Word of God in the world and, as well, with the tension between the life of the Church at any given point in the Word of God whose presence in the world the Church exists to hear, herald, and expose.

While the work of prophetism is characteristically associated with the laity rather than the priesthood, it is nevertheless true that where a congregation is a confessing community, and where, within a congregation, there is reliance on the Word of God and the Bible in preaching and in sacramental life, the very existence of such a congregation has a prophetic impact upon the secular life which surrounds it. For then the congregation represents to the world the life to which the world is called; then the life of the congregation prophesies the world which is to come in God's patience, judgment, and mercy.

Much the same thing as has been said about the laity's prophetic ministry to the world can be said about the other aspects of the service of the laity to the world.

Apologetics—the defense and explication of the Gospel against the world's hostility to the Word of God—accompanies the ordinary involvement of the laity in daily work in politics and business and culture. No Christian can get by very long in any kind of secular work or profession or activity without encountering the misconceptions which the world has about the Gospel, and without being exposed to the enmity which the world bears toward the Gospel. To be silent in the face of such perversion of the faith for such aggression against the faith is to become an accomplice. The laity cannot be saved from the apologetic tasks associated with their participation in the practical affairs of the world by the pronouncements of ecclesiastical authorities nor by the ministry of the clergy. Each layman must be his own apologist, responsible for his stewardship of the Gospel in his daily life and work.

. . . Witness becomes possible only when the Christian is on the actual scene where the conflict is taking place, the decision is being made, the legislation is being enacted.

Remember, though, that the witness made in the forums of public life is apt to be a secret witness, that not one which becomes known or openly recognized as Christian witness. It more and more appears to me that the Christian witness is exhibited dramatically in the world mainly when the congregation assembles for public worship. But when the members of the Body disperse into and within the common life of the world, the Christian witness is secret, known only to those actually involved in and reached by the witness being made, known only in the event itself, except as it becomes known to other Christians in the particular intercessions of the church for the world around.

And part of the stewardship of the Gospel by the laity in the world is intentionally, necessarily, and candidly evangelistic. It is the marketplace, as it has been pointed out, not the congregation or the premises of the Church, which is the place of evangelism. It is a work which cannot be done with fanfare—lest the uniqueness with which the Gospel addresses each man in his own life be vitiated. Nor is there some stereotyped scheme of evangelization. Evangelism is not essentially verbal, even though it seems commonly to be believed that the recitation of certain words constitute efficacious evangelism. Evangelism consists of loving another human being in a way which represents to him the care of God for his particular life. Evangelism rests upon the appeal to another man to remember his own creation—to remember Who made him and for Whom he was made. Evangelism is the event in which a Christian confronts another man in a way which assures the other man that the new life which he observes in the Christian is vouchsafed for him also.

The care which the Christian has for the world, the service of the laity to the world, is constituted in the very knowledge which is unveiled and praised in sacramental worship and preaching in the congregation: the Word of God is here and now among us in the world. The Christian life is a reliance upon that knowledge, a reliance lived among men, amidst all the powers and authorities in the world, in all things, in every place, at any time, in a way which discloses the presence of the Word of God to those who have not yet discerned Him in a way which affirms and loves that Truth about those who do not yet know Him.[1]

Lord Jesus Christ, teach me to do true evangelism; to know that "To be a witness does not consist in engaging in propaganda, nor even in stirring people up, but in being a living mystery. It means to live in such a way that my life would not make sense if God did not exist."[2] Amen!

Stringfellow, *Private and Public Faith*, 51–55.

Cardinal Emmanuel Célestin Suhard, quoted in L'Engle, *Walking on* 22.

FRIDAY

Quickly

You too must be patient and stouthearted, for the coming of the Lord is near. (James 5:8)

He who gives this testimony speaks: "Yes I am coming soon!" Amen! Come Lord Jesus. (Revelation 22:20)

The Church which is the holy nation is not metaphorical, but it is the Church called into being at Pentecost: the Church which is the new Israel of God in the world; the Church which is both progeny of the biblical tradition of Zion and pioneer of the kingdom of God; the Church which is the exemplary nation juxtaposed to all the other nations; the Church which as a principality and institution transcends the bondage to death in the midst of fallen creation; the Church which presents and represents in its corporate life creation restored in celebration of the Word of God; the Church in which the vocation of worship and advocacy signifies the renewed vocation of every creature; the Church which anticipates the imminent[1] and prompt redemption of all of life.

---

1. In many cases evangelical churches equate imminence and quickness, as in Revelation 22.

The Church's calling as the holy nation has been
profoundly distorted since Pentecost, and, manifestly, especially so under the aegis of the Constantinian détente
with the rulers and regimes of the present age. Insofar as
there was in the fourth century definite incentive to enter
that comity in order to alleviate persecution, the purpose
remains unaccomplished. If Christians have been spared
the savagery of beasts or if the more notorious vulgarities of emperor worship have been abated, other forms
of persecution have succeeded and the hostility of demonic principalities and powers toward the Church has
not diminished. By the twentieth century, the enmity of
the power of death toward the Church has come to be
enacted in the grandiose idolatry of the destiny of British
colonial imperialism, or in the brutal devastation of the
Church following upon the Soviet Revolution, or in the
ruthless Nazi usurpation of the Church in the name of
"Germanizing" or "purifying" Christianity so as to have
this accomplice in the pursuit and in the incineration of
the Jews.

Meanwhile, in America, the pluralism of religions
and the multiplicity of denominations have abetted the
inception of civil rights religion, which has assorted versions, but the major thrust of which imputes a unique
moral status to the nation, a divine endorsement for
America, which, in its most radical composition, disap-
propriates the vocation of Church as the holy nation.

Thus the Church becomes confined, for the most
part, to the sanctuary, and is assigned to either political
silence or to banal acquiescence. Political authority in
America has sanctioned this accommodation principally
by the economic rewards it bestows upon the Church.
The tax privilege, for example, to which the Church has
acceded, has been a practically conclusive inhibition to
the Church's political intervention save where it consists
of applause for the nation's cause

. . . It is a sign certainly of the demonic in institutional life where the survival of the principality is the
dominant morality. That mark is evident in very many
professed churches in America . . .

The suppression of the comprehension of the Church as the holy nation or as the priest among the nations, whether in America or elsewhere, causes, I think, the importance of the dispersion of the Church to be minimized or even overlooked. Yet it is impossible to contemplate the nationhood of the Church without retaining the sense of eschatological imminence . . .

The Church is episodic in history; the Church lives in imminence so that the Church has no permanent locale or organization which predicates its authenticity as the Church. This may seem a hectic doctrine of the Church to the Constantinian mentality. It is. But it is so because it suggests the necessity of breaking away from Constantinian indoctrination in order to affirm the poise of the Church awaiting the second advent of Jesus Christ.[2]

I pray for the Church, Lord Christ, and in praying for the Church, I find me praying for myself. Preserve me in your providence from skepticism, sarcasm, and sadness when I look at the Church. Remind me it is your Church and that I am an integral part and therefore open to correction and instruction. Amen.

2. Stringfellow, *Conscience and Obedience*, 102–4.

SATURDAY

Religion

Therefore, the Scripture says: "He ascended into the heights with captives in his train; he gave gifts to men." Now the word "ascended" implies that he has also descended to the lowest level, down to the very earth. He who descended is no other than he who ascended far above all heavens, so that he might fill the whole universe. (Ephesians 8:10)

Stringfellow had little time for religion, especially the American version, and was particularly hard on Protestantism, but Catholics do not get sway unscathed. He denounces religion as a human construct and he makes his case well, that we should rather be *incarnational* people, seeing God taking all initiative in history to make for himself, a people.

> . . . the central appeal of the mass evangelists was one of a radically individualistic religion, and in some instances there was [is][1] open distain for the Church as the Body of Christ in the world, as the holy community serving the world in the name of Christ. Here the emphasis is upon dignifying human sin as that which is responsible for the fallenness of not only men but the rest of Creation

1. Editor Mackey's insertion.

as well. So if men's work is harsh and burdensome, or if the authorities and principalities are relentless and oppressive, it is the fault of men and the consequence of sin. Are politics corrupt? Is alcoholism increasing? Is there scandal in the great corporations as well as in the unions? Does the nation's prestige decline? Are there more traffic fatalities? Is America losing the cold war? It is all because of the lusts of men. It is all because of individual sin. Repent. It will all change if enough repent. This is the stock merchandise of Protestant evangelism. Aside from other criticisms of this kind of religion, one trouble with it is that to extol the power of human sin, and particularly the efficacy of an individual's sin, is another way of asserting the dominion of men in the world. The focus of this religion is not the initiative of God in history, but the practice of religion by the individual in some singular, stereotyped act of personal volition and emotion by which a desired result can be achieved. This is a kind of inverse "positive thinking," and, one suspects, this is "positive thinking" for the lower classes.

In between these extremes of Protestantism, there is another version of the agnosticism of religion. It consists of a new social gospel which, though more chastened and cautious now than a generation ago, and though more orthodox in vocabulary (that is, nowadays Jesus is being called Jesus Christ instead of just Jesus), still expects that fortunate concurrence of circumstances in which men master history and build themselves a city of salvation. For such Protestants sacramental worship seems an indecisive, historically insignificant, and archaic exercise. And why shouldn't it if, from their vantage point, the saving work of God in Jesus Christ is incomplete and still contingent upon the work of men, and God is less than God? These are the Protestants who cannot, in other words, comprehend why the Gospel narrative does not end in the political triumph of Palm Sunday, not realizing that the event of Palm Sunday repeats in the life of Christ his temptation by the Devil in the wilderness. Consequently, of course, they cannot come to terms with the treachery of Judas and the apostasy of the rest of the disciples, nor countenance the Crucifixion, nor believe the descent into Hell, nor consider the Resurrection from the dead anything more but an embarrassing hyperbole.

The denunciation of the knowledge of God which is agnosticism, and which appears in various guises in American Protestantism, is not the only affliction visited upon the churches in the United States, nor the only form in which the hostility between American religious notions and the Gospel is evident.

Perhaps the most radical conflict between the American religious ethos and the Christian faith emerges from the proposition that in a society like the United States, within which there is a multiplicity of sects and churches and religious groups, it is not significant what a man believes religiously, or whether he is affiliated with any religious society or any denomination, so long as whatever his religious position is he adheres to it sincerely. It is not the content of religious belief or confession which is important, but the heartiness with which the adherent believes whatever it is he professes to believe. Faith, in this way, becomes faith in faith, not faith in God, nor even faith in some abstractions or hypotheses about God.[2]

Reverse any religious course or courses I may be plotting or indeed following; keep me Christian, knowing through faith that the incarnation of Jesus Christ is an act of God in history—in the common life of humanity into which I am invited through no schematic of my own creation. Make me return to my work, as the shepherds returned after seeing the babe in the manger, without thinking that I can add to or multiply the work God has already initiated. Amen!

2. Stringfellow, *Private and Public Faith*, 28–29.

WEEK IV

SUNDAY

I rejoiced when they said to me, "Let us go to the house of the Lord."
Now we stand within your gates, O Jerusalem: Jerusalem that is built
to be a city where people come together in unity. (Psalm 122:1–2)

And I saw the holy city Jerusalem, coming down out of heaven from
God, made ready like a bride adorned for her husband . . . (Revelation 21:2)

If modern men do not seem to listen to the Christian
faith or regard seriously the churches it is because the
churches have too often given men the impression that
they do not care about men or the world. They have
misled men into supposing that the Christian faith has
nothing to do with the ordinary issues of daily life.

But the issues of the world's life remain the issues of
the faith. No more persuasive and convicting, no more
beautiful and innocent evidence of that has been beheld
in this generation than the witness of Pope John XXIII,
noticeably beloved by the world. He knew that the cares
of the world are the responsibilities of the Church, the
concerns of the faith, are, in fact, the joys of the faithful.

So he left his throne to visit the poor in the slums of
Rome; he went to see the prisoners who could not come
to see him; he welcomed Jews as Joseph, their brother;
he blessed a circus. He was a pious, human, and humble
vicar of the Lord by being a servant of this world. All

Christians throughout the Church are called to a similar and equally simple service.

The Churches and the City: Witness to the faith means loving and serving the world. The city is the frontier today for the Church in American society. If the mission of the Church in representing the Gospel is to make an impact upon any sector of American life, it is to the city that the Church must turn and return.

The city is the frontier because the city not only increasingly dominates the whole of American society but indeed *is* American society. It is the place in which the realities present throughout the whole society have been congregated, concentrated, and brought into acute juxtaposition. Nearly half the population, for one thing, now actually live within the precincts of the modern urban complex. But those who live beyond those precincts do not escape the city's domination of commerce, culture, politics, and ideas.

If the social integration of races and nationalities is to be achieved in America the city will pioneer that achievement. If advanced technologies are to bring more freedom as well as more wealth to Americans, the city will be the first place to enjoy these benefits. If democratic government is a viable system for a mass society, the city will be the example of that. The city is the symbol of the American aspiration for freedom and society, the symbol—as the city has been for societies in the past—of salvation . . .

The notorious fact is that the churches at present do not *know* the city. And yet the rudiment of the mission to the city is the immersion of the churches in the common life and the dispersion of Christians within the turmoil and travail of the city's existence. The rudiment of mission is knowledge of the city because the truth and grace of the Incarnation encompasses in God's care all that is in the city. Mission in the city for the Church, and hence for all Christians, means a radical intimacy with every corner and every echelon of the city's actual life in order

to represent and honor God's concern for each fragment
of the city.[1]

I said: "Let me walk in the fields." He said: "No, walk in the town."
I said: "There are no flowers there." He said: "No flowers, but a crown."
I said: "But the skies are black; there is nothing but noise and din."
And He wept as He sent me back; "There is more," He said; "there is sin."
I said: "But the air is thick, and fogs are veiling the sun."
He answered: "Yet souls are sick, and souls in the dark undone!"
I said: "I shall miss the light, and friends will miss me, they say."
He answered: "Choose tonight, if I am to miss you or they."
I cast one look at the fields, then set my face to the town;
He said, "My child, do you yield? will you leave the flowers for the crown?"
Then into His hand went mine; and into my heart came He;
And I walk in a light divine, the path I had feared to see.[2]

1. Stringfellow, *Free in Obedience*, 18–22.

2. Prayer poem by William Blake, modified for singing by Beatrice Bush
Bixler.

MONDAY

Second Advent

But the truth is, Christ was raised to life—the firstfruits of the harvest of the dead. For since it was a man who brought death into the world, a man also brought resurrection from the dead. As in Adam all men die, so in Christ shall all men be brought to life; but each in his own proper place: Christ is the firstfruits, and afterward, at his coming, those who belong to Christ. Then comes the end, when he delivers up the kingdom to God the Father, after abolishing every kind of dominations, authority, and power . . . Listen! I will unfold a mystery: we shall not all die, but we shall all be changed in a flash, in the twinkling of an eye, at the last trumpet-call. For the trumpet will sound, and the dead will be raised immortal, and we shall all be changed . . . (1 Corinthians 15:20–23, 50–52)

Though the Word of God dwells in the world and is present within the common life of the world, not every man by any means knows or acknowledges that presence in history and in his own action and experience. Though the Word of God may be discerned in the passion and conflict of East Harlem gang society, for instance, that is no warrant that the very people within whose words and action the Word of God is hidden will see or hear the

Word, will understand the theological meaning of their own lives, will care about the knowledge of God given to them in and through their own concrete and everyday existence. And if a man cannot see and sense the Word of God within his own history, he will not have the eyes to see or the sense to realize, the presence of the Word in the larger history of the world or in the lives of other men or of nations, much less see any importance or relevance to the Church and the peculiar life of the Church in proclamation and celebration of the presence of the Word of God in the common life of the world.

The power to discern the Word of God is the mark of the Christian. It is not just one of an assortment of marks of the Christian; it is, in a sense, the unique mark essential to everything else which generally characterizes the Christian life. There can be no witness in the world to the Word of God by Christians individually or as the Church, save by the exercise of this power. There can be, of course, some witness to the Church, or to the churches, but neither of these is the same as the witness of Christians to the Word of God.

God witnesses to Himself in history whether or not there are Christians engaged in any witness to Him. The possibility of the witness of Christians as the Body of Christ and as members of the Body of Christ to the Word of God in the world depends upon the power given to Christians to discern the presence of the Word in the world. Further, and in the same fashion, there can be no worship, unless the power to discern the Word of God in the world is present. For how shall men worship that which they do not know? What is there to declare and present and celebrate, if the Word of God is not continually discovered and exposed in the life of the world? That which is called worship that is not consequent to the power to discern the Word of God in the world is not worship in the Biblical and Christian sense, but some superstitious practice, some foolish religiosity, some obscene idolatry.

The event of witness and the possibility of worship both originate in the power given to Christians to discern the presence of the Word of God in the world's common life.

Now if God's Word is present in common life, even though hidden except to the apprehension of faith, then the Word of God itself constitutes the essential and radical truth of common life and of every and any aspect of the world's existence at any and all times. It is in the Word of God that the secret of life is to be known. It is the Word of God that surpasses the dominion of death over the world's existence. The power, then, to discern the presence of the Word of God in the saga of the world's existence, reckoning with even the most puny human life, is saving knowledge. The power to discern the presence of the Word of God in common life is the gift of life itself, the restoration of life, the beginning of new life. The power to discern the presence of the Word of God in the world is the knowledge of the Resurrection.[1]

> . . . many of the people of the churches do not participate in this hope. . . these are a plethora . . . [which] signify a . . . bewilderment about the promise of Christ's second advent and skepticism about the veracity of Christ's resurrection. . . If there is no resurrection from death, Christians are to be pitied (cf. 1 Cor. 15:14).[2]

I believe in the resurrection of the dead—Christ first, then those who belong to Christ at his second coming. This is the only hope worth pinning one's life on—the only fact worth our efforts at believing. Keep me steadfast in this confidence, clear in this expectation, and faithful in this hope. Amen!

1. Stringfellow, *Private and Public Faith*, 62–63.
2. Stringfellow, *Conscience and Obedience*, 84–85.

Two Advents

We wish you not to remain in ignorance, brothers, about those who
sleep in death; you should not grieve like the rest of men, who have
no hope. We believe that Jesus died and rose again; and so it will be
for those who died as Christians; God will bring them to life with
Jesus.

For this we tell you as the Lord's word: we who are left alive
until the Lord comes shall not forestall those who have died; because
at the word of command, at the sound of the archangel's voice and
God's trumpet-call, the Lord himself will descend from heaven; first
the Christian dead will rise, then we who are left alive shall join
them, caught up into the clouds to meet the Lord in the air. Thus we
shall always be with the Lord. Console one another, then, with these
words.

About dates and times, my friends, we need not write to you,
for you know perfectly well that the Day of the Lord comes like a
thief in the night. (1 Thessalonians 4:13—5:1)

The biblical treatment of both advents, the narratives
attending Christ's birth and the testimonies about the
Second Coming of Christ, is manifestly political. Yet,

curiously, people have come to hear the story of the birth as apolitical and even antipolitical, while I venture, most listen to news of Christ coming again triumphantly with vague uneasiness or even outright embarrassment. What with the star and the sheep and the stable, it has been possible to acculturate the birth, to tender it some sort of pastoral idyll. But the scenic wonders, the astonishing visions, the spectacular imagery associated with the next advent have confounded the ordinary processes of secularization and thus the subject off the Second Coming has been either omitted or skimmed in the more conventional churches or else exploited variously by sectarians, charlatans, fanatics, or huckster evangelists.

Insofar as these allegations are sound, the mystery of both advents has been dissipated, whereas it is an affirmation of the mystery of both events that is most needed in order to be lucid, at all, about either advent.

So I begin by affirming the mystery of these happenings and, furthermore by noticing that what can be known of the two advents is no more than that evident in their biblical connections. It is the coherence of the one advent in the other advent, the first in the second and, simultaneously the second in the first, that is crucial.

Or, in other words, I do not know if, when Jesus was born there appeared a special star over Bethlehem, any more than I know whether, when Jesus comes as Judge and King he will be seen mid-air, descending amidst the clouds. Nor do I have need to know such things, they by no means control my salvation, much less the world's redemption. Yet, since both advents are mysteries, these styles bespeak those mysteries aptly, or so it seems to me.

There is a secret in the first advent, a hidden message in the coming of Jesus Christ into the world, a cryptic aspect in the unfolding of Christmas. Indeed, the biblical accounts of the birth of the child in Bethlehem, in such quaint circumstances, represents virtually a parody of the advent promise.

A similar discreteness—at times of such degree as to be ironical—marked the entire public life of Jesus Christ, according to the Bible. He taught in parables, finishing his stories enigmatically with the remark—*if you have ears that can hear, then hear* (cf. Matt. 1:1–23). When he healed a person or freed a demoniac he admonished witnesses to *see that no one hears about this* (as in Mark 7:31–37). When he was accused by the religious and political authorities, and confronted by Pontius Pilate, *he refused to answer one word, to the Governor's great astonishment* (Mark 15:3) . . .

Each advent of Christ is attended by mystery, what is now known of either event is not all that is to be known, but what is confessed by Christians as to both advents is known to them through the conjunction of the two.

That which is known and affirmed now because of the first advent and in the expectancy of the second advent is, however, enough to be politically decisive, that is to say, enough to edify choice and action in issues of conscience and obedience with respect to the rulers of the world. In the first advent, Christ comes as Lord; in the next advent, Christ the Lord comes as judge of the world and the world's principalities and thrones, in vindication of his reign and the sovereignty of the Word of God in history. This is the wisdom, which the world deems folly, which biblical people bear and by which they live as the church in the world for the time being.

The message which the life and witness of the church conveys to political authority, hence, always, basically, concerns the political vigilance of the Word of God in judgment. That news is, at once, an astonishment to all earthly rulers that Christ the Lord reigns already, as the first advent signifies, and as an anticipation of the destruction of all worldly political authority at the Second Coming.

Judgement—biblically—*does* mean the destruction of the ruling powers and principalities of this age. I am aware that this is, for professed Christians in America and in many other nations, an unthinkable thought even though, it be biblical (1 Cor. 15:24–28; cf. Acts 2:34–36; Rev. 18–20).[1]

---

1. Stringfellow, *Conscience and Obedience*, 76–80.

God, I need the discernment only you can give to keep a faith and witness within the tension between the first and the second Advent. Don't allow me to drift into apathy or to atrophy in a passive, convenient faith; keep me vital in remembrance and faithful in expectancy. Amen!

WEDNESDAY

Uniqueness of Jesus

For there is one God, and also one mediator between God and men, Jesus Christ, himself man, who sacrifices himself to win freedom for all mankind, so providing, at the fitting time, proof of the divine purpose... (1 Timothy 2:5–6)

... if wisdom is the knowledge of God as a gift and if Jesus Christ epitomizes that gift, what is to be thought of the historic religions of men? Are they to be dismissed because they do not so regard and honor Christ? Are they to be suppressed as enemies of the Gospel? Are their adherents to be proselytized because they are pagans or are they to be shunned as unbelievers? Or, as some would have it, is the Christian faith essentially undistinguishable from the religions? Is some common element to be found both in the Gospel and in the religions that diminishes the importance of any differences between them? And what of all the other varieties of religious belief and commitment common to men—the personal conceptions, notions, motivations, and, sometimes, superstitions, even hallucinations—which constitute the actual faith of many persons? Is there some kind of equality among the hosts of religions, both the great and popular ones and those merely individualistic, and the ancient ones as well as those which survive today, which means that one religion is as valid or efficacious as another? Is religion anyway such a private affair that inquiry into the comparative claims of the various faiths is precluded? Is it arrogance that underlies the much repeated assertion of Christians that there is something unique about their faith that sets it apart from all other faiths?

As the term is intended here, religion is an art in which men contemplate and inquire into the nature of ultimate reality and in which, through speculation, reflection, meditation, and discipline, men conceptualize and, more or less, systematically formulate their convictions so derived. Further, it is an attempt to prove or defend the truth and efficacy of their views, to discern and try to apply the implications of these views to personal existence and life of the world, insofar as there may be such implications, and invent, institute, and practice rituals and observances that express their allegiance to the conception of ultimate reality that they have made, found, inherited, or otherwise accepted.

Religion, thus, is a human enterprise presupposing the existence of some god or gods or principle or force or object which has moral significance in some way for men in this world, whether that be fear of punishment, purpose, a promise of immortality, a claim of righteousness, assurance of happiness or whatnot. Religion claims significant insight into those characteristics of the existence of ultimate reality, however defined or conceived, which provide guidance for men in seeking and establishing relationships with that existence. What is known in this world of ultimate reality or god consists of what men have discovered, learned surmised, deduced, or guessed from their own intellectual, emotional, physical, and spiritual efforts.

There are very great qualitative differences between the formal and institutionalized religions of mankind, past and present, and the little, private religions with which some men satisfy themselves. The content of the former varies substantially in comparison one with the others, and the content of the latter varies with each religionist. On top of that, in each of the historic religions, sects, and factions abound with their particular interpretations of doctrine, distinctive ritual practices, and separate pietistic exercises. Yet for all the variances, all these forms of religion hold a common methodology; all share in the same essential approach to the religious issue. All consider religion as the human quest for God. All have confidence in the capacity of men, or at least, of some men, to breach the mystery of God. All emphasize human initiative in establishing relationship with divinity. All focus upon some conception of God as the object of devotion, the source of meaning, and the determination of moral behavior.

It is exactly at this point—not necessarily in content, but in method, that the Christian Gospel is radically distinguished from all religions. The theme of the Gospel from the first moment of the Fall . . . is God in search of man. The emphasis is upon the initiative God takes toward men in the world. God volunteers relationship with men. God gives himself for all mankind. What men may know of God is only that which God himself discloses for men to know.

Thus the confession of faith characteristic of Christians, since the times of the Apostolic and Nicene Creeds, does not propound any idea or conception of God, but bespeaks, just as the Bible does, God's living presence and action in this world. The religions aspire to describe the attributes of God; the Gospel proclaims God's accomplishment in this world in meeting men where they are. It is upon this difference between the religions and the Christian faith that any responsible claim of uniqueness for Christianity rests, and not, as people of the churches have so often and so fondly supposed, because God prefers Christians to other men.[1]

God, I fear that, without a conscious awareness of the Word of God, I may think myself, my church, a recipient of your special attention. Remind me often that there is no preferment in Christin truth,

---

1. Stringfellow, *Count It All Joy*, 27–29.

and that I belong to the creatures called "humankind," and therefore because of this, and this alone, I am a recipient of God's grace. Amen!

THURSDAY

Victor

All that came to be were alive with his life, and that life was the light of men . . . (John 1:4)

". . . God be praised, he gives us victory through our Lord Jesus Christ" (1 Corinthians 15:57). Though the clash between Christ and the principalities in his trial and execution is the decisive and normative encounter, it is not at all the only occasion in the historic ministry of Christ when he is confronted by the principalities. The final showdown is again and again foreshadowed in Christ's life on earth.

The apprehension with which he is regarded by worldly authorities during the Palm Sunday celebration and during Holy Week is first exposed in the consternation and rage with which Herod received the news of Christ's coming into the world. At the same time, remember that it is part of the authentic miracle of Christmas that those who gathered at the stable to adore him do so as representatives of the whole of creation, as emissaries of all men and all creatures and all things. Those who come to worship and honor Christ in his birth include the Magi, who come as ambassadors of the principalities of the world. For a moment, as it were, in the Christmas event the sovereignty of Christ over all the world is revealed, and it is in that event that the world has a glimpse of the very restoration of creation from the fall, a foretaste of the world become the Kingdom of God.

The Lordship of Christ is disclosed in the adoration in the Christmas miracle, but the hysteria and hostility of Herod at Christ's coming into the world foreshadows the later encounters between Christ and the principalities. The time of Christ's temptation in the wilderness as a particularly significant episode has already been mentioned. But, in addition to that, Christ confronts the principalities when he stills the tempest, heals the sick, frees the demoniac, upsets the tradition of Israel by eating with sinners, or shows that he is Lord of the Sabbath. And, Christ's wilderness temptation is repeated on Palm Sunday. Yet that is not the last encounter between Christ and the principalities, for he goes to cleanse the Temple, and Lazarus is raised from death. Then, betrayed and forsaken to death by the disciples, condemned to death by the rulers and crucified and buried, he descended into hell—into the event in which the presence and power of death is most militant, pervasive, ruthless, and undisguised.

In some of the episodes, as in the wilderness, the crucifixion, and the descending to hell, death openly confronts Christ; in others, Christ is visited by one or another of the principalities as emissaries of death. In all of these encounters, the principalities represent the awesome and manifold powers of death.

The victor in each specific encounter is Christ. That is important because it means that the power of Christ over death is not merely a transcendence of death as the terminal experience or as biological extinction. Thinking of the resurrection is having reference only to the crucifixion and entombment of Christ[1] underlies the wistful, vain, and false ideas about the immortality of the soul or life after death which so violate the gospel and corrupt the minds of many church people. Each specific confrontation between Christ and death and between Christ and

---

1. The terminal event of his earthly life.

one of the principalities as one of the powers of death foreshadows the resurrection, exposes and heralds the overwhelming authority over death which Christ has and holds from the beginning of time to the end of time. And the resurrection encompasses and represents all of these particular historic encounters in a single, consummate, and indeed cosmic disclosure of the triumph of Christ over death.

The resurrection is impregnated with all that has gone before; these encounters of Christ with death and its powers in history mean that his triumph over death there shown is offered for men and for the whole world. His victory is not for himself, but for us. His power over death is effective, not just as the terminal point of man's life, but throughout his *life*, during this *life* in this world, right now. This power is effective in the times and places in the daily lives of men when they are so gravely and relentlessly assailed by the claims of principalities for idolatry which, in spite of all disguises, really surrenders to death as the reigning presence in the world. His resurrection means the possibility of living in this life, in the very midst of death's works, safe and free from death.'

But what of all these notions and speculations about life after dying, after the day of the undertaker? The Christian, the man living by the authority of and in the freedom of the resurrection, is saved from fond and wishful thinking about that. The Christian has no anxiety about his disposition after his life in this world: in fact, he knows little or nothing about the matter; but he knows all that he needs to know, which is that the reality and truth of the resurrection has been in the present life so radically verified and realize that he is confident and joyful in leaving himself in the judgment and mercy of God, in all things, forever and ever . . . In Christ is both the end and fulfillment for all principalities, for all men, and for all things.[2]

Keep me, Lord Christ, from the idols of history and my com-mon life in the world. What you have done you will complete; what

2. Stringfellow, *Free in Obedience*, 70–73.

you have said has been said; what you have declared over me is as good as done. Remind me often of the incomparable power of the Bethlehem birth—and of those present there; they in a very real sense included me. I am grateful. Amen!

FRIDAY

Word of God

. . . though by this time you ought to be teachers, you need someone to teach you the ABC of God's oracles over again; it has come to this, that you need milk instead of solid food. Anyone who lives on milk, being an infant, does not know what is right . . . (Hebrews 5:12–13)

Commitment to the Word of God manifests in a hunger for and a love of that Word. Advent centers "upon the significance of the Bible for Christian people and for the life of the Church." Stringfellow forces us to reflect on our Bible study practice, for it is in such an act that we find both the first and the second Advent.

> Some . . . were appallingly diffident toward the Bible, and those who were the most self-serious about the analysis of culture and society were most often dilettantes in Bible study. Those professing condolence for people showed mostly indolence for the Bible. Apparently, some of the clergy felt that Bible study was unnecessary, since they had already learned all they needed to of the Bible in seminary.
>
> To some others in the group ministry—and to myself—this seemed astonishing in the extreme, especially among Protestants who might be expected to recall that, historically, Protestants have been a people of the Word

of God in the Bible. Surely, intimacy with the Word of God in the Bible, reliance upon the Word of God in the Bible, is a characteristic of the ordinary practice of the Christian life, it seemed to those of us who urged that the group ministry and the people of the congregation engage in some corporate Bible study each week. After much controversy about the matter, it was decided that the group would spend an hour or so in Bible study just before the regular weekly staff meetings. It was often an erratic, sparsely attended—or attended to—exercise, but it exposed the fundamental disunity within the group ministry as to the content of the Christian faith and the nature of the Church's life and work. In this Bible study, the minds of some were filled with notions of truth, ideas of good, with interesting hypotheses, strong sentiments, and current events—and these things were actually asserted to test the Word of God. But few seemed ready to just *listen* to the Word of God in the Bible, to ask: What *is* the Word of God? Now, later, much later, after many struggles and both indifference and resistance, with the counsel and nurture of such visitors to the parish such as Suzanne de Dietrich, Hendrick Kraemer, and others, the Bible has been acknowledged as central in the life of the Church and, hence, of this parish—but only after much agony."[1]

That such agony is experienced in our relationship to the Word of God both drives us to pray for Christ to return and, at the same time, to question, wonder, and examine whether we, as the Church, are listening to the Word of God or merely talking over it.

At the heart of the conflict and disunity regarding the place of the Bible in the Church—as in many other churches outside Harlem—was a fundamental misapprehension about what the Bible is . . . None of these approaches to the Bible essentially affects the reliance upon the Bible of the ordinary Christian as a particular means through which the Word of God is uttered and may be heard by men no less today than in the earlier days of

---

1. Stringfellow, *My People Is the Enemy*, 92–93.

the Christian people. In other words, and without denigrating an appropriate place for Biblical scholarship and criticism, the characteristic approach to the Bible of the Christian is confessional. The Christian confronts the Bible in the expectancy that it is in and through the testimony of the Bible of God's presence and action in the common life of the world that he will behold the Word of God as such, that he will hear the Word of God in the objectivity, integrity, and serenity of God's own witness to Himself in this history, that he will confront the *living* Word.[2]

Perchance particular notice should be given to the usage . . . of the phrase *the Word of God.* I intend this to be understood as a name. Thereby I refer not only to the Bible as the Word of God, but simultaneously, to the Word of God incarnate in Jesus Christ, and, also, to the Word of God militant in the life of the world as the Holy Spirit, and further, to the Word of God inhering in the whole of creation.[3]

In all the wonder that adheres in Advent, our being confronted with the presence of the Word of God—yes, confronted with it in all its breadth and fullness of meaning—is what is meant to be our experience—Christians being confronted with being Christian.

From the softening trappings of pre-Christmas, which strike us ubiquitously the day after All Hallows' Eve, deliver me. Keep me from becoming familiar with the world's ways of falling into Christmas headlong, and grant that an Advent of living in the Bible will find me formed by the Word of God, to which I give allegiance. Amen!

2. Stringfellow, *My People Is the Enemy,* 93.
3. Stringfellow, *Conscience and Obedience,* 14.

CHRISTMAS EVE

Before God and before Christ Jesus who is to judge men living and dead, I charge you solemnly by his coming appearance and his reign, proclaim the message . . . with all the patience that the work of teaching requires. (2 Timothy 4:2a, c)

. . . there is never an abstract, single, "Christian answer" to an issue to which all Christians are bound to adhere or conform. On the contrary . . . positions taken by [those] . . . implicated in an actual case, [were] all responsible Christian positions.[1] Christians care that every man be evangelized . . . care for all of society . . . care for all men in a radically individual sense and are free to advocate the cause of one [or another].

The image of Christian action in the world is that of the people of God living in dispersion in the world and in any corner of the world, finding trustworthy God's promise that He cares for all men and for each man. Moreover, Christians are free in their dispersion to intercede for the cause of any man—even on who is said by others to be unworthy—and thereby to represent to the world the intercession of Christ for all men—even though none be worthy. The image of the Christian witness in the world is that of a people who have so

---

1. Stringfellow is referring to a specific issue, of course, but the editor has omitted this to emphasize the *principle involved.*

completely divested themselves of their own individual self-interest that they may intercede—stand in the place of, represent, advocate—the cause of another, any other at all. And then, now and again, the people return from their extraordinary versatile involvement in the life of the world, to gather as the Church to represent, before God, the world, out of which they have come, in all concreteness and conflict and change, and to celebrate as the Church the presence of the Word of God as they have known it in the world.

If the life of the Church, either of the members dispersed in the world or of the gathered worshipping community, is to be an exercise of the power to discern the presence of the Word of God in common life and is to be a radically free and versatile involvement in the turmoil and travail of the world's everyday existence, if the life of the Church is to be intercessory; and if the Church is to be the servant of the world in the name and in the style of Christ, then Christians must live in the world—and not for their own sake, and not for the sake of the Church, much less for the sake of any of the churches, not even for God's sake, but for the sake of the world. That is to say, the Christian must live in this world where Christ lives; he must live in the world *in* Christ.

Yet what Christians are faced with are churches . . . which at every echelon of their existence—Sunday school, youth fellowships, vestries and sessions, agencies, councils, denominations, congregations and parishes, women's work, rummage sales, bingo games and coffee hours, sermons, seminaries, boy scouts, choirs and dial-a-prayers, bastard architecture, segregated premises, effete or effeminate images of Jesus, grossly inflated bureaucracies, and all the rest—church, which are to a great extent separated from the world, afraid of the world, which feel unprepared, insecure, and inadequate for the mission of the Church in the world, and for whom the jargon of theological discussion or the examples of the clergy or the formalities of the practice of religion are no assurance or adequacy. These churches more and more retreat into themselves. They become so inverted, so caught up in the internal maintenance and procedures, so entrapped in preserving and proliferating a cumbersome, costly, self-serving, officious, indulgent, soft ecclesial apparatus that it becomes easy to think that they don't have to care about the world any more since they are so much consumed in caring for themselves.

Nevertheless, it is when and where the churches are most estranged from and least involved in the common life of the world that the churches are the most worldly, and most resemble the worldly principalities and powers. The separation of the churches from the world, the superstition that the Word of God is or can be isolated from the ordinary, everyday life, the preoccupations of the churches conserving their own existence rather than serving the world—all these are the substance of estrangement from Christ. Where the churches do not care for the world, they do not really care for Christ.[2]

Deliver us from being defined by our ecclesial hierarchy, be we laity or clergy. Whatever vows we have taken, we will obey for you, Lord Christ; wherever there is room for discernment, let us discern— but keep us ever caring first for the world, that we may care for you. Amen!

2. Stringfellow, *Private and Public Faith*, 73–75.

BIBLIOGRAPHY

Ellul, Jacques. *The Presence of the Kingdom*. Translated by Olive Wyon. Philadelphia: Westminster, 1951.

L'Engle, Madeleine. *Walking on Water: Reflections on Faith and Art*. New York: Convergent, 2016.

Stringfellow, William. *Conscience and Obedience: The Politics of Romans 13 and Revelation 13 in Light of the Second Coming*. Waco, TX: Word, 1977.

————. *Count It All Joy: Reflections on Faith, Doubt and Temptation*. Grand Rapids: Eerdmans, 1967.

————. *Dissenter in a Great Society: A Christian View of America in Crisis*. New York: Holt, Rinehart, and Winston, 1966.

————. *Free in Obedience*. New York: Seabury, 1976.

————. *My People Is the Enemy: An Autobiographical Polemic*. New York: Holt, Rinehart, and Winston, 1964.

————. *The Politics of Spirituality*. Philadelphia: Westminster, 1984.

————. *A Private and Public Faith*. Grand Rapids: Eerdmans, 1962.

————. *A Simplicity of Faith: My Experience in Mourning*. Nashville: Abingdon, 1983.